D1192225

Benjamin E. Mays and Margaret Mitchell:

A Unique Legacy in Medicine

Mays, President Benjamin E.
Morehouse College
Atlanta

Atlanta, Georgia
June 29, 1942

Dear President Mays:

I have received your letter of June 22nd, requesting that I give a tuition scholarship of $80 to Morehouse College and that I consider making this an annual donation. I am enclosing a check for $80 and I hope it will be of assistance to some fine and deserving student. I am sorry that I cannot promise to make this an annual contribution. The uncertainty of the future based on the war as well as the heavy demands upon me make it impossible for me to promise to do any more.

Whenever I have made any donation to any cause or organization, I have done so with the understanding that no publicity of any type would be given to my contribution. I am sure you understand the reasons behind this and I hope you will keep this matter confidential.

Sincerely,

(Margaret Mitchell)

Mrs. John R. Marsh

Text of Letter Accompanying the First Tuition Scholarship Donated by Margaret Mitchell to Morehouse College

Benjamin E. Mays
&
Margaret Mitchell:
A Unique Legacy in Medicine

by

Ira Joe Johnson and William G. Pickens

FOUR-G Publishers
1996

LC
2851
.M72
J65
1996

Copyright ©1996 by Ira Joe Johnson
Printed in the United States

All rights reserved. No part of this volume may be reproduced without the written permission, in advance, of the author.

FOUR-G Publishers Cataloging-in-Publication

Johnson, Ira Joe
Benjamin E. Mays and Margaret Mitchell: a unique legacy in medicine / by Ira Joe Johnson and William G. Pickens.

140 p. 22 cm.

ISBN 1-885066-08-2 (pkb.)
ISBN 1-885066-09-0 (hardcover)

1. Morehouse College (Atlanta, GA.) --Funds and scholarships. 2. Mays, Benjamin E. (Benjamin Elijah), 1894-1984--Correspondence. 3. Mitchell, Margaret, 1900-1949--Correspondence. 4. Smith, Otis Wesley, 1925- --Biography. 5. Afro-American physicians--Scholarships, fellowships, etc.--Georgia--Atlanta--History. 6. Afro-American dentists--Scholarships, fellowships, etc.--Georgia--Atlanta--History. 7. Afro-American college students--Scholarships, fellowships, etc.--Georgia--Atlanta--History. I. Pickens, William G. II. Title.

LC2851.M72 J65 1996

Published by:
FOUR-G Publishers, Inc.
P. O. Box 2249, Winter Park, Florida 32790
(407)679-9331

TABLE OF CONTENTS

DEDICATION

This book is dedicated to:

The memory of Dr. Benjamin E. and Sadie G. Mays and their neice Cordelia Blount.

The memory of Mrs. Margaret Mitchell Marsh and John R. Marsh.

Dr. Otis W. Smith, my mentor and friend.

My wife, Ruby, whose love and encouragement has been sustaining, and to our children -- Ira Joe, Jr. (Joey), Tamara Janelle (Tammy) and Ivan Jeffrey (Jeffrey).

My parents, Rev. Hardy and Plueanna Carswell Johnson and the Johnsons and to my wife's parents, Rev. Charlie and Lucille Wright and the Wright family.

PREFACE

We were guests on the same television talk show, Dr. Otis Smith and I, when our paths crossed in 1991. He tipped his straw hat and looked me in the eyes and said, "Young lady, I know who you are and I have a story to tell you about Margaret Mitchell that you won't believe."

I knew who Otis Smith was. As President of the Atlanta chapter of the NAACP, he was well known. What I didn't know at the time was the rest of the story.

It took us about six months before we finally got together. We met for lunch, and the conversation went on for hours. What he told me touched my heart and a close friendship evolved that has led the two of us -- a black doctor and a white journalist -- along a curious path back into Atlanta's history.

To understand the significance of the journey, you have to return to the 1930's. Otis was a young black boy growing up in a poor neighborhood in a segregated Atlanta. As he nursed his dying father, who was unable to get proper medical treatment, he vowed that one day he would become a doctor.

Margaret Mitchell, the daughter of one of Atlanta's pioneer families, had just published a book called <u>Gone With the Wind</u>. It became an overnight bestseller, and its author, a world renowned celebrity. She had written a book about Atlanta during the Civil War and Reconstruction. The theme was "gumption" -- a quality that separates those who survive adversity from those who don't.

Smith was a newspaper boy when Mitchell's novel and then its Hollywood version put Atlanta on the map. In fact, he kept a scrapbook of newsclippings about the Atlanta author. Smith went on to other jobs, harvesting crops in summer months, to pay his way through college and eventually medical school. But, it wasn't enough.

When he confided in his mentor, Dr. Benjamin E. Mays, that he couldn't return to Meharry Medical School for his second year because of lack of funds, Dr. Mays cautioned Smith not "to do anything rash" and to come back to see him in a couple of days.

Dr. Mays, the son of former slaves, was President of Morehouse College. When Smith returned to his office, he quietly assured him that his entire medical education was paid for on the condition that he return to Georgia to practice medicine when he finished his training.

Years later, Smith, by then a doctor, visited with Mays and asked who was responsible for his scholarship? Mays told him the name of his sponsor, who was then dead, and swore him to confidence.

As we met for lunch, Dr. Smith and I, on a spring day in 1992, he told me the rest of his story. He returned to Georgia in the 1950's where he practiced pediatrics for forty years. His influence spread beyond the state, however, when he led the movement to integrate the nation's public hospitals. As President of the Atlanta chapter of the NAACP, his leadership inspired other blacks to break through barriers to realize their own dreams.

So here we are today, Dr. Smith and I and another Morehouse graduate and Mays' protege, Ira Joe Johnson. Together we have collaborated to unravel the mystery of Dr. Mays' close relationship with the author of the Civil War era novel, Margaret Mitchell. This granddaughter of former slave owners in the North Georgia hill country and this son of former slaves conspired to insure the undergraduate and medical education of scores of young black men, including a young newspaper boy by the name of Otis Smith.

Ira Joe Johnson's manuscript tells a compelling story of collaboration between a black man and a white woman during a period in Atlanta history marked by massive segregation and heightened racial tension. Mays and Mitchell are dead, but their legacy lives on. Ira Johnson's dogged persistence has uncovered the stories of black doctors across America who owe their medical education to Margaret Mitchell and who vowed to take this knowledge to their grave.

The Pittsburgh Courier printed a column written by Dr. Mays shortly after Mitchell's untimely death in an automobile accident in 1949. "She was simple and modest," he wrote. "Her fame and popularity did not go to her head. The people who knew her intimately loved her dearly."

Every few decades, history has a way of rewriting itself. Ira Joe Johnson's research offers a new perspective on Margaret Mitchell, who Mays described as "perhaps the greatest author the South has produced." Was he referring to the author or the woman or both? This work allows the reader to draw his or her own conclusions.

Mary Rose Taylor, Chairman
The Margaret Mitchell House
Atlanta, Georgia

FOREWORD

Hardy Ivy started Atlanta, but William Tecumseh Sherman, with the help of a little lady, put it on the map. That little lady was Margaret Mitchell, creator of Scarlet O'Hara and Rhett Butler. The June 28, 1936, issue of the Atlanta Constitution, gave the world notice of the imminent publication of Gone With the Wind in an advertisement, announcing its cost of $2.75. Sure enough, by June 30 Margaret Mitchell was autographing her "just off the press" ten year effort in the book shop of Davison-Paxon Department Store on Peachtree Street. And Atlanta, the South, and the world would never be the same. That the world was ready for Gone With the Wind was evidenced when the writer's husband, John Marsh, announced in December 1936 that the sales had hit the "million mark, " after just six months! This story is told in my Atlanta and Environs: A Chronicle of its People and Events, 1954.

On July 30, 1936, only one month after the book's publication, David O. Selznick purchased the motion picture rights to it for $50,000. The premiere of the movie took place on Friday, Dec. 15, 1939, in the Loew's Grand Theater on Peachtree after Vivien Leigh and Clark Gable led the sensational parade to the site. Lined up six deep along Peachtree Street, Atlantans and Georgians of all ages, shapes and hues strained to get a look at the stars of the movie about the book which nickels and dimes had purchased and placed on a shelf next to the Holy Bible in many a home. Bands played and searchlights combed the skies. Atlanta has not seen such a spectacle since Sherman's unforgettable, incendiary passage of sixty years earlier.

Margaret Mitchell had been born Nov. 8, 1900, of an old substantial Atlanta area stock, running back "five generations on the paternal side and four on the maternal side." Her parents were Eugene Mitchell and Maybelle Stephens Mitchell. The family resided in a house on the Northeast corner of the Boulevard and Forrest

Avenue, the latter street named after General Nathan Bedford Forrest, the scourge of the Yankees and originator of the Ku Klux Klan. Margaret grew up to become fascinated with the Civil War and thoroughly knowledgeable about it, as the book attests.

In 1940, a tall, handsome, black man, Dr. Benjamin Elijah Mays, returned to Atlanta as president of a small, impecunious college begun in Augusta in 1867 as a grade school for ex-slave males. Oddly enough, the path of the black college, its president, its students, and the author of Gone With the Wind would cross in ways that are little known and to the credit of both. Correspondence between Margaret Mitchell and Dr. Mays shows that she has taken a kindly, though surreptitious, interest in helping Morehouse College graduates from pre-medical and pre-dental programs manage their expenses once they arrived in professional schools. The story can now be told because Morehouse College graduates Ira Joe Johnson, William G. Pickens, and George C. Grant have been working toward that end. White House liaison Ira Joe Johnson, who had been a very close friend of Dr. Mays, came into possession of the letters. He called upon Morehouse Professor and Former English Department Chair Pickens to assist with the editorial responsibilities and upon George Grant to publish the story.

It is a thrilling story that warms the cockles of the heart of how Dr. Mays and Margaret Mitchell reached toward each other, aided and abetted by her husband John Marsh, to help raise the level of health care in her home state and beyond by assisting in the education of numerous black doctors and dentists-to-be who were, as Dr. Mays could easily demonstrate, in need. Here they speak of how they were helped, not knowing the true source until recently, and what they have done with their highly successful health careers.

I applaud this captivating work and urge you to buy and enjoy it.

Franklin Garrett, Atlanta, Georgia

INTRODUCTION

They were two southerners, a black man and a white woman. She heralded from an old-line, aristocratic, Atlanta family with a prominent name and wrote a famous novel that became a celebrated movie. She had a yearning passion to help the needy. He heralded from parents who were dirt poor sharecroppers. He had a yearning passion to gain an education and help his fellowman. She wrote one book; he wrote nine. Her book, the best-seller, Gone With The Wind, illuminated and eulogized the Old South. His autobiography, Born to Rebel, demonstrated a black man's ability to cope with the legacy of the Old South and to go on to do memorable and important things. The paths of these two southerners were destined to cross, and they did. They learned to work together for the good of the South and the nation.

The phenomenal ascension of Gone With The Wind in 1936 to the pinnacle of creative literature during its era gave Margaret Mitchell the power, prestige and "bully pulpit" to advance causes that were designed to heal, not to divide. The phenomenal growth of predominantly black Morehouse College between 1940 and 1967 speaks volumes for the dynamic leadership of Benjamin Elijah Mays. His causes were designed to heal and to arouse.

When General William Tecumseh Sherman thoroughly defeated the South, the Civil War ended; but the battle for the hearts and souls of the southern people was just beginning. The publication of Gone With The Wind stimulated battles. It unleashed a legion of new political debates and sociological diatribes in cities and hamlets of the North and the South. The tensions growing from the Civil War, Reconstruction, disfranchisement, lynching, sharecropping, convict leasing, Jim Crow law and practice were palpable to the white majority and also felt in the daily lives of the black minority. For Whites, ironically, Gone With The Wind gave them back their pride. They now felt vindicated and victorious. For Blacks the book posed problems.

The purpose of this book is not to revisit the political correctness of Gone With The Wind nor stir the passions of either its supporters or detractors. Whether Gone With The Wind is seen as a true representation of the Old South, an intrepid indulgence of historical myths, a misrepresentation of characters that cast sadly the images of poor southern Whites, and at the same time maligned and further perpetuated the stereotypical notions that the nation had about Blacks, or whether it was merely one of the best romantic novels of all times is not to be debated or determined in this book.

What is pertinent to the theme of this book is the fact that Margaret Mitchell, in the 1940s, following the international triumph of her novel and equally successful movie, could have written her ticket to virtually any place or position in the world. The President sent invitations from the White House; prime ministers and potentates sent diplomats to her door; and emissaries wired cables inviting her abroad. Hollywood and the literary world were already hers, having seen her novel win the prestigious Pulitzer Prize in 1936 and the film based on her novel win nine Oscars (Edwards 295) and the title of "Best Picture" at the Academy Awards in 1940. At the very least, the conservative Daughters of the Confederacy would have given her a ready forum and welcomed her into its ranks as spokesperson. After all, her pivotal role in telling the world about Scarlet O'Hara and Rhett Butler, magnolias and Tara, and the battle for Atlanta gave her the proverbial key to all southern cities. She was then and is now the Premier Southern Daughter, the Belle of the Ball.

The intriguing aspect of Margaret Mitchell's life is that she chose neither of these waiting opportunities to exploit her fame or increase her fortune. Instead, while she cast her lot on the side of numerous causes, one of her causes had an unusual focus: the improvement of medical conditions in her beloved South. In the end, she became a pioneer in race relations by giving her time and money to helping young Morehouse men both during their undergraduate years at the historic black institution and also while they pursued their medical and dental degrees at Meharry Medical School in Nashville, Tennessee, and Howard University School of Medicine in Washington, D.C. Mitchell cast her considerable clout and wealth, anonymously, on the side of medical assistance for Blacks and the poor. She did this in unison with, and at the persistent urging of Morehouse College president, Benjamin Elijah Mays. Mitchell's money and Mays's vision resulted in significant support for the education of over twenty black doctors, some of whom are profiled in this book. Mitchell went further and stimulated the building of a hospital in Atlanta for its middle-class black citizens.

What follows is that story.

Ira Joe Johnson

ACKNOWLEDGEMENTS

We gratefully acknowledge the contributions of many of our friends, mentors and associates, who were kind enough and interested enough in ensuring that this book was completed that they rendered invaluable service to this endeavor.

Special thanks to Dr. Otis Smith and Mrs. Gwen Smith for assisting in identifying and contacting many of the Mays - Mitchell Scholarship recipients and to Dr. Clinton Warner and Mrs Sally Warner, whose resources supported the success of this project.

A heartfelt thank you to Mary Rose Taylor and Noel King at the Margaret Mitchell House, Inc. for providing materials and support to the preparation of this book.

Additionally, this book could not have been completed without the support of Attorney Warren Fortson, Executor of the Benjamin E. Mays estate; Attorney T. Hal Clarke, Executor of the Mitchell Estate; and Attorney Hughes Spalding, Jr., Senior Partner, King and Spalding.

Our warmest expressions of appreciation to the late Robert Johnson, Senior Executive Editor of Jet Magazine, for his timely insights and advice as we began this project.

We are eternally indebted to the staff of the Archives at the University of Georgia for their extensive research assistance in documenting the content of this book.

A sincere debt of gratitude is owed to April Thompson and Tonette Manley for their invaluable assistance in the preparation of memoranda, questionnaires and the manuscript.

Ira Joe Johnson

ACKNOWLEDGEMENTS

My personal thanks to the staff of the Morehouse College Computer Center, Edward Williams, Natasha Benson, and Wilson Rice and Gail Mitchell at Clark Atlanta University for their important technical assistance.

Words of appreciation are due the staff at the Robert W. Woodruff Library at the Atlanta University Center; the staff at the Fulton County Library; and Janice Sykes and Gloria Mims of the Auburn Avenue Branch Library for supporting this research.

Further debts of gratitude are due all my children -- Leslie, Reese, Todd and Marcus; and especially to my wife, Dr. Ernestine W. Pickens, who read and critiqued the manuscript also.

And, I am eternally grateful to co-author Ira Joe Johnson who invited me to participate in this project.

William G. Pickens, Ph.D.

And, finally, a word of thanks to FOUR-G Publishers, Inc., for its faith, guidance and professional assistance in the planning, preparation and publication of this timely book.

I
THE STORY

This is the story of the South's most famous daughter, Margaret Mitchell, rising from antebellum Atlanta wealth and social standing. She joined hands with the son of proud, tenacious, God-fearing former slaves of South Carolina over fifty years ago with the singular mission of financially assisting Morehouse College students in their quests to become doctors. It is indeed fascinating to learn from the letters between Mays and Mitchell that twenty years before Dr. Martin Luther King, Jr. delivered his famous "I Have A Dream" speech, in which he pleaded for a day when "the sons of former slaves and the sons of former slave owners will one day be able to sit down together at the table of brotherhood," Mitchell was already a full partner with Dr. Mays and his mission to save a weakened Morehouse College from extinction. She wrote her first check to the black institution and sponsored the first scholarship for a needy student in 1942. Her continued commitment and generosity increased substantially over the next several years. This commitment helped make it possible for students to be admitted to Morehouse college early, that is, from the tenth or eleventh grade, under a plan devised by Mays. Thus, twenty-two years before Dr. King's speech, Margaret Mitchell had not only sat down at the table of brotherhood, but at Morehouse she had picked up the check.

Benjamin Elijah Mays was born on August 1, 1894, in a rambling, four room shack on the outskirts of Ninety-Six, South Carolina, near the town of Epworth, the eighth child of former slaves, Hezekiah and Louvenia Mays. Born near the turn of the century, Mays entered a world of legal segregation, where racism was rampant and the lynching of Blacks for even the smallest infraction of Jim Crow laws and established racial customs was as common as Saturday evening baseball and picnics on the Fourth of July. Certainly, the spectacle of a black man hanging from the largest, most visible tree was considered casual fun and a gamey sport with plenty of fireworks; and the admission was free. More Blacks were lynched at or near the turn of the century than at any other period in history. Dr. Mays wrote in Born to Rebel that one of his earliest recollections was that of a white mob harassing his father:

> *I remember a crowd of white men who rode up on horseback with rifles on their shoulders. I was with my father when they rode up, and I remember starting to cry. They cursed my father, drew their guns and made him salute, made him take off his hat and bow down to them several times. Then they rode away. I was not yet five years old, but I have never forgotten them.* (Mays 1)

For as long as Mays lived, every fiber of his being was shaped by his conception of a loving God, a ready recollection of that hate-filled mob, and a desire to achieve at a high level with his students doing likewise.

The fact that Mays was able to rise above the chains of racism and hate is a great testament to the eighty-nine and one-half years of his life. Samuel Dubois Cook, president of Dillard University and a Morehouse alumnus, states, "The life of Dr. Mays was the life magnificence, the life lived fully at the summit, on the dazzling mountain top, the life of the impossible possibilities, the life spent in persistent pursuit of the unattainable ideal, the impossible dream." Eulogizing his beloved teacher and mentor, Cook praises Mays for his spiritual vision and his independence:

> *Mays was born free. He lived free. He died free. Always courageous, he was a prophet to the core of his being--always emphasizing the creative tension between the "is" and the "ought," promise and fulfillment, the Kingdom of*

man and the Kingdom of God. He was always his own man (Inquirer 5)."

Mays was heavily involved in the Civil Rights Movement. As early as 1923 he had defied Jim Crow laws, to the great consternation of white passengers, by seeking to integrate a Pullman coach in Birmingham, Alabama, for a trip to St. Louis. He was required, at gun-point, to change to a Negro coach. According to another Morehouse alumnus, Noel C. Burton, Mays took a revolutionary stance at the college. Burton states, "Sedition was hatched in the chapel. The revolution was sown on Tuesday mornings in the chapel on the Morehouse campus." He adds that Mays waded into injustice unmercifully in those gatherings (385). Among those who sat before Mays and listened intently was Martin Luther King, Jr. Later, Mays, a friend of the King family, became a close and supportive counselor to King.

In a tribute entitled "The Last of the Great Schoolmasters," Lerone Bennett, Jr., Morehouse alumnus, referred to Mays as the vanguard of the Civil Rights Movement. "Mays was bold enough, wise enough and selfless enough to assume the awesome responsibility of bridging the gap between the first Reconstruction and the second." Bennett added, "None tilled more ground or harvested a more bountiful crop than Benjamin Elijah Mays, a lean, beautifully-black preacher-prophet who served as Schoolmaster of the Movement (Bennett 74-79)."

The life of Benjamin Elijah Mays was an odyssey of prayer, faith, hope and opportunities created by his sheer will and determination to make his mark in the world. It was an indelible and honorable mark! Raised in a family with a father who had no tolerance for the lofty ideals of education, Mays attended school only four months of each year and did not graduate from high school until age twenty-one. The prevailing racial conditions that forced his father to bow before a white mob were the same conditions that prevented Mays from casting his first vote until age fifty-one. In 1916, he graduated from high school at State College in Orangeburg, South Carolina, as valedictorian of his class. Never satisfied with mediocrity, Mays set sail on an academic course of excellence that took him to Bates College in Lewiston, Maine, where he earned the coveted Phi Beta Kappa key in 1920, though it was withheld until 1935. He received his M.A. in 1925 and his Ph.D. a decade later, both from the University of Chicago.

Although Mays had been Dean of the School of Religion at Howard University, he spent most of his academic life at Morehouse College. President John Hope hired Mays in 1920 as a mathematics teacher and debate coach of the all-male institution. Always the pursuer of excellence, mentor and motivator, Mays set high standards for his students both in mathematics and debating. He had more than one run-in with the administration because of his strict grading habits and high expectations for his students. The story goes that a late-comer to class would probably find the door firmly locked. Two of Mays's debating students, James Nabrit and Howard Thurman, went on to become nationally known decades before Mays's best known student, Martin Luther King, Jr., ever gained national recognition. James Nabrit, a prominent civil rights attorney, helped Thurgood Marshall in his landmark Brown vs. Board of Education case, the case that eventually led to desegregated schools in the South; and Howard Thurman became the most noted theologian of his era. We may confidently surmise that there is not a theology school in this country, black or white, that has not utilized books written by Thurman and Mays.

On August 1, 1940, on his forty-sixth birthday, Mays began the first of twenty-seven years as the sixth president of Morehouse College. And the appointment could not have come at a better time for the seventy-three year old institution. Although Morehouse enjoyed a reputation as an excellent school for educating the best, the brightest, and the most affluent black males, the college was on a fast track towards bankruptcy and ultimate closing. The academic buildings and the entire plant facilities were in urgent need of repair; faculty pay was less than it was at the other schools of the Atlanta University Affiliation, and resignations were rampant. Students paid tuition haphazardly; and, what was most humiliating of all, Morehouse students had to get their meals from the campus cafeteria at another institution, Atlanta University.

According to Orville Vernon Burton, Mays faced a forbidding task. Burton writes,

> *Mays found morale low, the endowment on the point of losing a million dollars, and the school in the least favorable position among the colleges that formed the Atlanta affiliation* (Burton 28).

Morehouse, 'the stepchild of the affiliation,' was 'fast becoming a junior college.' Atlanta University controlled Morehouse's budget and finances, Morehouse students ate meals on the Atlanta University campus, and Spelman provided medical care for them (28)."

Margaret Mitchell's parents were Eugene and Mable Mitchell. Eugene was a lawyer and her mother a staunch suffragette. Margaret's great ambition was to finish Smith College, go to Vienna to study with Sigmund Freud, and then become a psychiatrist. This dream she told her fiance, Clifford West Henry, according to Ann Edwards, before she was eighteen (Edwards 47). She neither finished Smith nor married Henry nor traveled to study with Freud nor became a psychiatrist. But O! What a mark she made in the world anyway! Mitchell preferred to be called Peggy, not Margaret. She had a "worldly sense of humor and ribald conversation" plus a "salty tongue and feminine charm," writes one of her biographers (7).

Mitchell's childhood was filled with stories and lore about the Civil War. Edwards reports that Mitchell was taught the names of

Civil War battles along with the alphabet, and she went to sleep to her mother's "doleful Civil War songs" (21). At the age of four, she attended a Confederate parade (20). At five she regularly rode her pony alongside the horse of a Confederate veteran who was a friend of the family (24). By age ten she began writing stories of a romantic bent (30). After Margaret finished high school, Maybelle wanted her to finish a fine New England college, Smith, in Northampton, Massachusetts. Maybelle took her daughter there and enrolled her. Maybelle did not live very long afterwards. Margaret did not find great success at Smith, so she went home after the freshman year to become lady of the house and care for her father (61).

Clifford Henry, Mitchell's first beau, had military duty and died in combat (54). Margaret, a great flirt, had no trouble attracting men. She met two other young men interesting to her, Berrien Upshaw and John Marsh. She married Upshaw first, with Marsh as best man, then divorcing him, married Marsh. This marriage to Marsh was one of the most fortuitous developments of her life, for he worhipped the ground she walked on. Marsh encouraged her to write, so Mitchell wrote short stories, one of them, fittingly, about the Confederate generals memorialized in sculpture on Georgia's Stone Mountain.

Marsh was a journalist, working for the Atlanta Georgian. She became a journalist too, working as a feature writer for the Atlanta Journal. Upon Marsh's constant urging that she write a novel, telling her that if she wanted something to read she would have to write it, Margaret reluctantly began a novel in 1926. Ten years later it would be Gone With The Wind. John felt a responsibility to critique and edit her writing so that it would be clear and precise and also to keep her writing (140).

When the manuscript was finally finished, Harold Latham of Macmillan took an interest in it and coaxed Mitchell to give him the manuscript (Pyron 301). Lathan read it and vowed that Mitchell was "the best story teller he had ever encountered in his job (Edwards

170). He genuinely liked the manuscript. On publication day, there was "mayhem" at Davison-Paxon's bookstore. Edwards writes: "Customers were tearing books out of each others' hands (208). Mitchell had to work very hard thereafter to avoid the demands of an adoring public and those who wanted to share her wealth. Later, David O. Selznick bought the movie rights to Gone With The Wind for $50,000. The premiere was a marvelous thing. Co-author Pickens tells about it:

> *It was December 15, 1939, and I was ten years old. My seamstress aunt, Aunt Nene (Christine Houston), who with Bro. Oliver, her husband, reared me after I was orphaned at age nine, walked me from Felton Drive, from where I was born in Grady Hospital, to Peachtree Street. The occasion was the parade with many celebrities in town for the premiere of Gone With The Wind. My aunt's excitement infected me too. We wanted to see the celebrities. People from limping elders to babes in arms headed up all of the streets-- Forrest Avenue, Baker, Cain, Ellis, Houston, Auburn Avenue, Edgewood, Decatur--toward Peachtree Street.*
>
> *We reached the east side of Peachtree Street by way of Forrest Avenue and started inching away from the direction of the segregated Fox Theater past Davison-Paxon's department store toward the segregated Loew's Grand Theater. The crowd was soooo thick and soooo noisy. I held my ears and strained to see, going regularly on tiptoe because of the big people in front of me. My aunt held my hand to keep us from becoming separated. The searchlights were fascinating as they played on the sides of buildings, criss-crossed in the air like they were playing a game of tag, and then shot up to scan the skies, as they would do increasingly with World War II coming nearer and nearer. The crowd surged ahead; the parade was on! Steadily moving left, as we could, we saw the*

open car, saw Clark Gable! saw Vivien Leigh! saw Mayor Hartsfield! and the rest! We stood still, craning our necks to see everything!

Afterwards, we walked home fast, exhilarated. A few days later Aunt Nene called me into the dining room, where she and Bro. Oliver kept a small library in a corner. She pulled out a large paper back book from a position next to the Bible and said, "This is Gone With The Wind. I want you to read it. It's all about the Civil War." I did.

The Marshes, like Margaret's parents before her, and many Whites in Atlanta and a few Blacks, had a history of hiring house servants. The Marshes had Bessie and her daughter, Deon, the two of them handling the cooking and cleaning; Eugene Carr, the janitor; and Carrie Mitchell Holbrook, the laundress (65-6;336). The Marshes had no chauffeur/ gardener, it appears. John had begun to have heart attacks requiring hospitalization, distressing developments for Margaret; but she nursed him conscientiously at the times he had releases from the hospital. At other times, one or the other of the servants would become ill also and require her attention. In 1946 Carrie Mitchell Holbrook became terminally ill with cancer and needed a hospital in which to die. Even though the Holbrook family had the means to pay, Carrie's race denied her access to a single private hospital in Atlanta. Only Margaret's intercession, and an "anonymous" donation from Margaret, persuaded the sisters of Our Lady of Perpetual Help to admit Carrie for her last days of life (321). Margaret became fully aware of the plight of sick African Americans in deeply segregated Atlanta and would not forget it. The contrast between John's easy access to private hospitals and her own, as compared to Carrie's, was stark.

Movie lovers, the Marshes decided one day to go to see "The Canterbury Tales" at a theater on Peachtree Street. John was freshly out of the hospital, and Margaret, who usually drove, helped him out of the car. As they crossed the street toward the theater, reaching the middle, a fast-moving car came at them. Leaving John, Mitchell moved backwards toward her own car, and the wayward car followed her. Fatally injured, she lingered in the hospital a few days and died (Edwards 335). Before she died, however, she had been influenced by Dr. Benjamin E. Mays.

When Mays took the helm at Morehouse, he knew that he had to raise money by any legitimate means necessary. By 1941 World War II was already threatening the enrollment at the college, for many young men were being drafted or feeling the need to volunteer. Mays had promised to give "to Morehouse College all that I have... the best of my mind, heart, and soul. I will give...my money until it reaches the sacrificial point." He had said, "I will serve this institution as if God Almighty sent me into the world for the express purpose of being the Sixth President of Morehouse College (Burton 29). To save Morehouse, Mays instituted policies which required strict tuition payment, earning him the nickname, "Buck Bennie." He raised the faculty pay and embarked upon a $400,000 endowment fund-raising campaign that ended in the construction of several new buildings (Rovaris 52). Mays needed more help. He decided to broaden his appeal to the wealthy, thinking, at some point, of Margaret Mitchell. Mays had thought that whites would give freely to Morehouse but had been sorely disappointed. He was obviously taking a chance by asking this Southern Daughter for money for that reason and because Margaret Mitchell's standing in the black community was shaky indeed. Many Blacks felt Gone With The Wind, book and movie, to be discriminatory and resented what they considered the accommodating spirit exhibited by some black leaders at the time of the movie's premiere (52).

Blacks were criticized for the small part they played singing outside the majestic Loew's Grand Theatre, which was bedecked in white columns that sought to depict a slave plantation named Tara and bedecked also in Confederate flags. Besides, they sang outside the

City Auditorium, at which the Gala Ball was held. Some Blacks were unhappy about Black participation of this sort. For example, the president of the local N.A.A.C.P., T.M. Alexander, critical during the time of the event, spoke vehemently against the "accommodation" of his people. Alexander, recalling the period later, wrote that Blacks "had dressed in antebellum and slave costumes" to sing in front of these places that they could not enter. Alexander characterized these actions even at the time as "offensive to Blacks and stinking to high heaven" (Beyond the Timberline (212). The situation was such that Hattie McDaniel, who later won an Academy Award for her role in the movie, refused to come to Atlanta for the premiere even though the South was willing to make an exception for the black woman selected to play the role of "Mammy." McDaniel did not want to face the necessarily segregated and therefore sub-standard accommodations which would be provided for her. Perhaps setting the stage for future aid to Blacks, Mitchell let it be known that she was dismayed that Hattie McDaniel, "a real star," felt it necessary to turn down Atlanta's offer to attend the premiere because of the deplorable Jim Crow laws in her city (Edwards 288). Mitchell must have felt that at some point and in some way she would make amends.

Mays sharply felt a need to expand the circle of friends of the college. He went after Margaret Mitchell, a wealthy woman who was interested in her home city. The first set of letters between the two served to introduce Mays to Mitchell and to begin the solicitation process. In the first letter, dated October 15, 1941, Mays told Mitchell that at its Seventy-Fifth Anniversary, Morehouse College stood at a crossroads. It must raise $400,000 on or before June 30, 1942, in order to receive matching funds. Mays was pointed: "We want you to help us." One week later he received a reply which seemed positive from John Marsh, Mitchell's husband: "I will be glad to have you telephone me in order that we may arrange an engagement." By November 11, following a conference with John Marsh, Mays was making another appeal to Mitchell, adding a wish that she would speak to the students. He was aware that in the black community there were still those who resented deeply some aspects of the novel and the movie.

Perhaps Mays felt that if Mitchell visited Morehouse, introduced by him to a receptive Morehouse student body, that event could have done wonders for her image and helped the college. So Mays extended a cordial welcome to the novelist and at the same time asked for a donation. Marsh responded, "I cannot offer much encouragement as her list of contributions and donations for 1941 was made up some time ago." Marsh tried to close the door on the idea of Mitchell's visiting the campus: "She is not a speech-maker and never has been....She does not agree with the current belief that writing a novel...endows a person with oratorical ability" (11-11-41).

Mays was undeterred. His response, addressed to John Marsh, was, "I...understand the many demands or requests for donations. I can only say that Morehouse is worthy of her help, that the College has existed here in the heart of the South for seventy-five years and that we feel that the Atlanta public should give its endorsement of an institution which for seventy-five years has served the Negro race and through that the South" (11-24-41). By the next June, Mays apparently decided that a more direct approach of asking for a specific sum might work. He reminded Mitchell of the initial request of the year before and said, "I am writing now in a slightly different vein." He mentioned that the enrollment was between three-hundred-fifty and four-hundred men. He told her that until recently he had had money for only one $40 scholarship a year for a deserving student, but now he would have $440. He added, "We give scholarships without having money to back them up.... "I am wondering if you would give one tuition scholarship of $80." He would like it to be an annual gift (6-22-42). Mitchell answered, "I am enclosing a check for $80.... and commented that "no publicity of any type" should be given to her contribution" 6-29-42). Thus, with this gift, Mays had begun to accomplish his purpose of gaining financial support from Mitchell for Morehouse.

Mays reports to Mitchell that the $80 was used both to help "a young man deserving help who had achieved an average of 3.80 and to help the college to"close the year out of the red." He adds, though, that the war has cut the college's enrollment from 400 to 200 (5-10-43). Mitchell follows through as Mays must have hoped: "I was glad to have your letter telling me of the excellent record of Charles W. King.... I am enclosing a check for eighty dollars, to be awarded to the student you and the Board of Trustees feel to be most deserving of aid in this coming year." She leaves it to Mays to decide how the money will be used: "[P]lease use your own judgment" (5-24-43). Two summers later, Mays writes Mitchell to say that the college met its budget for the previous year but needed help for the current year: "If the persons who gave scholarships last year will give the same amount this year...we will close June 30, 1945, in good shape again." He mentions the need to raise $330,000 in endowment funds to be matched by the General Education Board." He ends with a request for a further contribution (7-6-44), and Mitchell promptly sends a check for $100 (7-18-44).

By May of 1946, Mays knows of Mitchell's plan to establish a memorial fund at Morehouse to be used specifically "to further medical education among Negroes" (10/23/46). Mays points out the strength of the college's pre-medical and pre-dental programs, "thus enabling our students to enter first-class medical schools without being handicapped." Mays supplies Mitchell with a calculation of the costs involved in the pre-professional programs, identifies the two medical schools for Negroes and their costs, and makes a comparison with the costs at white Indiana University. He knows that Mitchell prefers that any of her assistance in the medical area go to students who plan to practice in Georgia, but Mays prefers a broader latitude. He states: "Any part of the south may be just as much in need as Georgia or Atlanta" (5-8-46). Mitchell is very busy during this period caring for her ailing husband and has little time for the question of scholarships, locations, and plans. Therefore, Mitchell's response to Mays came months later.

In October 1946, Mitchell's correspondence shows that her contribution to Morehouse received a boost from a black woman's will. Carrie Mitchell Holbrook, the laundress for the Marshes, willed her money to them (Mays 212). Mitchell tells Mays that she wishes to provide aid to Morehouse "in honor of a Negro friend, Carrie Mitchell Holbrook, who died last spring." She notes that Carrie's nephew, Grady Bennett, is a student at Morehouse on the GI Bill and wishes to be a doctor, a wish that Carrie shared. Mitchell writes, "Years ago we promised Carrie that we would see to it that Grady was assisted in getting the best medical education possible." Mitchell tells Mays that she has arranged with the trust officer at the Citizens and Southern National Bank to monitor $3000 for Bennett's medical education, and she encloses legal papers which give Mays discretion about how to use the money in case something happens to prevent Bennett from receiving a medical education (10/23/46).

Apparently, it was the Holbrook will that had stimulated Mitchell to give more money to Morehouse, specifically to assist potential doctors. She encloses $2000 to Mays, also in memory of Carrie Mitchell Holbrook, to be used "to assist a deserving student in acquiring medical and dental education," the student to be chosen "on a basis of character, good will toward their fellow man, and willingness to work, rather than on brilliance or high scholastic grades alone." Before conceding on the question of where the young man that she assists should practice, an impassioned Mitchell decides to share with Mays her dream. She tells him, "I see the desperate need in Atlanta and in Georgia. I believe I know this need more than the average white person not in social service work, I want to better my own state.... We are poorer in Negro doctors, I am sure, than almost any other state." She continues:

> *It is very disheartening to those who try to do something for the upbuilding of their state and section to see the smartest brains drained off from the South to crowded Northern sections.... The time will come when Atlanta will*

> *be the largest Negro city in the south, the time will come when we will have a large, and, I hope, famous Negro hospital for training boys and girls from this section. When that time comes, I hope we will have excellent Negro doctors in this section to staff this hospital."*

Then comes the concession: "Still, if circumstances indicate that practice in some other Southern state is necessary for the livelihood or happiness of some young Negro doctor, I would hate to feel that I had stood in the way. So I must leave that to your discretion." She closes, "[B]ut I ask that you make very clear to anyone who accepts this money... that it would be the wish of Carrie Mitchell Holbrook that they stay here and help their own people" (7-8-46).

In that most important letter, Mitchell, trusting Mays, had made a commitment to the education of young black doctors which still reverberates around the country. Mays wrote to Mitchell to suggest that the most effective use of the $2000 would utilize the matching support of the General Education Board by assigning the money to the college's endowment. The matching funds would raise the total to $4000 whose income would help a student in medical school. "Then your work and that of Mrs. Holbrook," he adds, "would live on indefinitely" (11-1-46). Mitchell agrees with the matching plan (11-7-46). Mays thanks her (11-13-46) and in the next spring lets her know of his need to raise the endowment to $2,000,000 (3-14-47). Mays adds in the letter that it will be four months before he writes her again because of obligations to the United Negro College Fund. His letter two weeks later is strictly informational. He sends a copy of the statement relative to the Carrie Mitchell Holbrook Memorial Fund which will go into the next catalog of the college, asking her approval (5-28-47).

He writes to the Marshes in the fall of the next year to report that with their help the endowment has successfully reached $2,000,000 and he must turn now to the physical plant (11-9-48). Mays's next letter turns out to be the last one written while Mitchell was alive. In it he tells the Marshes that after July 15, 1949, he will be working on the campaign of the United Negro College Fund but that in the fall he hopes to launch the $3,000,000 endowment campaign for Morehouse. He indicates that he "can not afford to lose the interest of" a single donor and hopes that future donors will be as committed "as [she} has been in the past" (3-12-49).

In addition to helping the pre-professional students at Morehouse, Mitchell gave money for founding a medical facility for middle class blacks in Atlanta. Mitchell had always been interested in the medical field, always with a consciousness of health care matters. She found herself caring for her ailing father and husband during lengthy periods. Also, various family servants needed her personal care. She was in a series of accidents and suffered several illnesses. And, she volunteered for the Red Cross.

The one public hospital, Grady, had a small unit for Blacks. A few years after the October 23rd letter to Mays, Mitchell sent a check for $1000 and a letter to Hughes Spalding, Sr. who was just beginning work on a plan to add a public unit for Blacks to St. Joseph's Hospital (4/17/46). Mitchell, conscious ever of her struggle to find a private, paying hospital willing to accept her dying laundress, Carrie Mitchell Holbrook, wrote a recommendation in her letter that Spalding study the possibility of starting a private hospital for Blacks.

Mitchell's contribution and support resulted in the construction of the Hughes Spalding Pavilion. Spalding gave her full credit in a letter to Mitchell's brother after she passed suddenly. Mays participated in the naming of the hospital after a committee narrowed the list to three names: Margaret Mitchell, Charles Drew, and Hughes Spalding. Mays not only assisted in naming the hospital, but in 1950 he spoke at the dedication of the new building. Eventually, Mays entered his final rest from a private room at Hughes Spalding Pavilion on March 28, 1984.

It is not altogether surprising that Dr. Mays sought the help of Margaret Mitchell. With both being avid readers and risk-takers, their paths might have crossed twenty years earlier when Mays was professor, debate coach, and pastor in Atlanta and Mitchell was an ambitious, unorthodox, bright and promising reporter with the Atlanta Journal. Neither Mays nor Mitchell was comfortable "toeing the line" within the social boundaries of the status quo. She was raised by a family of notable stock and comfort, the daughter of an attorney father who was president of both the Atlanta Bar Association and the Atlanta Board of Education, and an educated, history-conscious mother. Although Mitchell's life was one of "pedigreed prominence," she never allowed her social standing to get in the way of her impulsive nature, bold independence, or her dreams.

In her book entitled Margaret Mitchell and John Marsh--The Love Story Behind Gone With The Wind, Marianne Walker wrote about an incident in which young Mitchell demonstrated bold independence. She, dressed in a sexy Apache costume, and her partner performed what was then termed a lewd dance at a predebutant affair sponsored by the Junior League. The performance created a stir among old and young socialites in Atlanta and resulted in Mitchell's exclusion from the imminent and prestigious debutante ball. Needless to say, Mitchell was hurt by the snub but decided to get even one day (Walker 34). With her book she received the acclaim of all, which in a way was sweet revenge for Mitchell. Margaret Mitchell, a multifaceted personality who always marched to the beat of a different drummer, proved to be just the type of southerner to heed Mays's call for help to support the needy Morehouse College. Although their relationship was a unique alliance, it allowed both Mitchell and Mays to show their rebellion against their milieu, she toward social restriction and he toward racial proscription. Their collaboration to improve the educational and medical opportunities for black men was indeed one of many strange fruits of the South's "peculiar institution." Mitchell's unexpected death in 1949 ended the collaboration.

Margaret Mitchell in April, 1936, one month before publication of Gone With The Wind.

Photo courtesy of the Atlanta History Center

Dr. Benjamin E. Mays,
President, Morehouse College, circa 1942

Photo courtesy of Morehouse College

Dr. and Mrs. Mays, in 1951, at Their 25th Anniversary

John R. Marsh in 1952

Photo courtesy of the Atlanta History Center

Margaret Mitchell with a copy of her 1936 Pulitizer Prize winning novel, Gone With The Wind

Photo courtesy of the Atlanta History Center

Margaret Mitchell with Her Father, Eugene M. Mitchell

Photo courtesy of the Atlanta History Center

Dr. Benjamin E. Mays with Author Ira Joe Johnson at the 1991 Dedication of the Benjamin E. Mays High School in Atlanta.

Dr. Benjamin E. Mays, with Godson, Ira Joe Johnson, Jr. and Author, Ira Joe Johnson, Sr.

Dr. Otis W. Smith, Vice Chair, and Mary Rose Taylor, Chair, Margaret Mitchell House, Inc., in Stuttgart, Germany.

Photo courtesy of the Margaret Mitchell House, Inc.

Former Daimler-Benz North America Chair and CEO, Edzard Reuter, Mary Rose Taylor and Dr. Otis W. Smith, with Plans for Renovation of the Margaret Mitchell House

Photo Courtesy of the Margaret Mitchell House, Inc.

The To-Be-Restored Margaret Mitchell House.
(She lived in the Tiny First Floor Apartment At the Lower Left From 1925-1932, Where She Wrote Gone With The Wind.)

Photo courtesy of the Margaret Mitchell House, Inc.

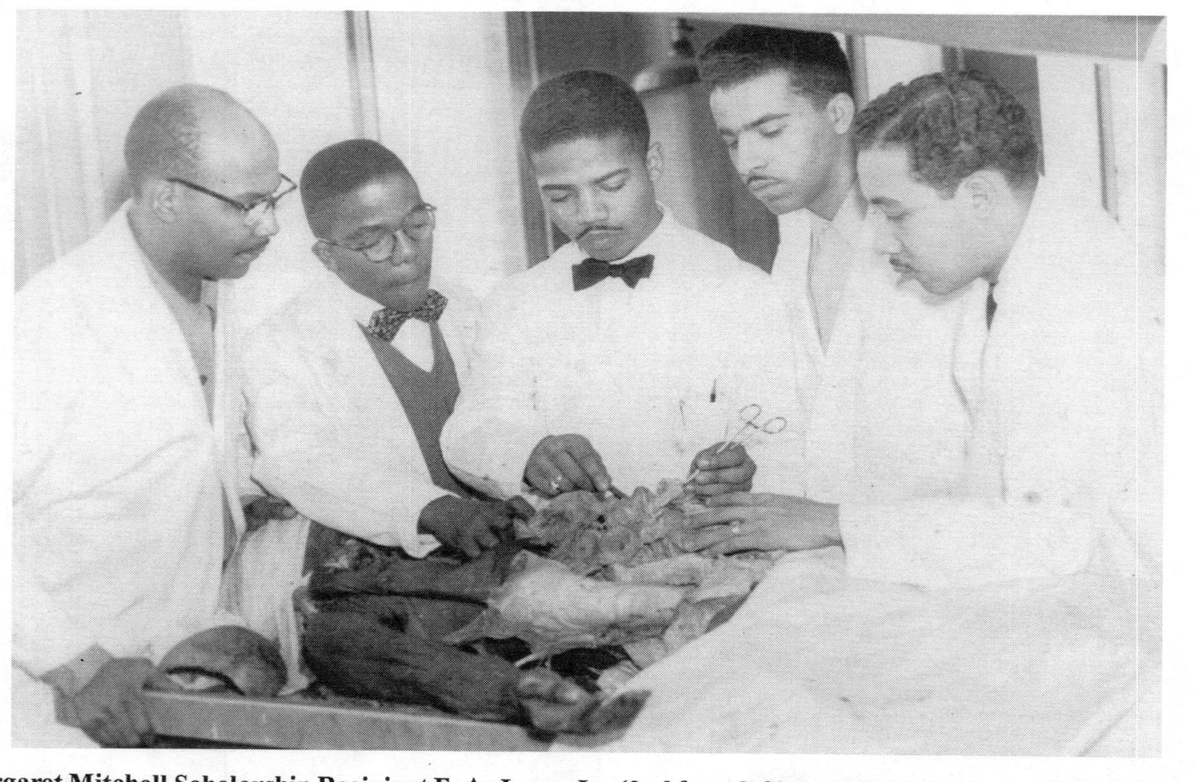

Margaret Mitchell Scholarship Recipient E. A. Jones, Jr., (2nd from left) and other Morehouse College Alumni (l-r) J. Arthur Kelly, Sowell Harris and an unidentified student in an Anatomy Class at Meharry Medical School with Instructor, Morehouse College Alumnus Calvin Calhoun.

Morehouse College Alumni at Meharry Medical School in 1951.

Graves Hall, Morehouse College, circa 1936

Courtesy of Morehouse College

Sale Hall, Morehouse College, circa 1936

Photo courtesy of Morehouse College

Science Building, Morehouse College, circa 1936

Photo courtesy of Morehouse College

Campus View with Robert Hall on Right and Sale Hall in Background, circa 1936

Photo courtesy of Morehouse College

Campus View, Morehouse College, circa 1936

Photo courtesy of Morehouse College

II
The Letters

After Margaret Mitchell sent the first scholarship check to Dr. Mays in 1942, there was a need to select the recipient. Mays and the Morehouse Board of Trustees, true to the Morehouse tradition, wanted a student whose academic credentials were impeccable and whose personal character was unquestioned. Obviously, Charles W. King was felt to be that kind of student, one who represented W.E.B. DuBois's "talented tenth," one who was academically driven and determined to find success. Mays wrote to Mitchell:

> *We have just held an annual meeting of the Board of Trustees of Morehouse College, and the members of the Board want me to express our appreciation to you for your scholarship contribution.*
> *It enabled the college to award a scholarship of $80 to Charles W. King, a young man deserving help who would have had a very difficult time making it through the year without your aid.* (5-10-43)

Mitchell responded:

> *I was glad to have your letter telling me of the excellent record of Charles W. King. I am glad that my donation went toward helping him through this past year.... I am enclosing a check for eighty dollars....* (5-24-43)

It was clear that Mitchell was leaving it to Mays and the college to determine who the scholarship recipients would be. Mitchell added: "...if you feel that there is some other student who needs it more, please use your own judgment." Three years later, Mitchell felt she should state her preference. Wanting her assistance earmarked for medical or dental students, she wrote:

> *And now, about this check for $2000 which I am enclosing--it also is given in memory of Carrrie Holbrook. I want it used to assist deserving students in acquiring medical and dental education. I think that I may speak for Carrie, as well as for myself, when I say that both of us would prefer the students to be chosen on a basis of character, good will toward their fellow man, and willingness to work, rather than on brilliance or high scholastic grades alone.* (10-23-46)

Character rather than brilliance was what mattered most to Mitchell. This preference seems characteristic of Mitchell's life. A common thread woven in her life, aside from her reverence for war patriots and her sense of duty, was the many disappointments she and her husband had with medical doctors. She often said that it meant more for a physician to show compassion, kindness, and understanding for the patient than just to rely on some medical formula without a bedside manner. So, the future Morehouse doctor should be not only smart but also courteous and compassionate. On this subject, like many others, Mitchell and Mays shared the same philosophical values. Mays often said, "It is not good enough for Morehouse to develop men brilliant in mind and articulate in speech but men who are honest."

For more than fifteen years, October 1941 - 1957, an intriguing trail of correspondence transpired between Benjamin E. Mays and Margaret Mitchell Marsh and/or her husband, John R. Marsh. Scattered among their letters are related correspondence from scholarship recipients, financial advisors, and others connected to the story of the Mays-Mitchell legacy. The letters that follow documents these hereto fore little known acts of great compassion which had a major influence on the lives of countless Americans.

October 15, 1941

Mrs. John R. Marsh
1268 Piedmont Avenue, N.E.
Atlanta, Georgia

Dear Mrs. Marsh:

Morehouse College is celebrating its Seventy-Fifth Anniversary and this means that for seventy-five years this institution has stood here in the heart of the South and Atlanta developing men to serve the Negro race and the nation.

We come to this Seventy-Fifth Anniversary facing an uncertain and somewhat precarious future. We are in the midst of a campaign to raise $400,000, which amount must be raised on or before June 30, 1942, in order to meet certain conditions of getting this amount matched. We want you to help us.

May I phone you for an appointment sometime during the week of October 27? I would like to have the opportunity to talk with you about this institution.

With kindest regards and requesting an affirmative reply, I am

Sincerely yours,

Benjamin E. Mays
President

BEM:MLB

October 21, 1941

Dr. Benjamin E. Mays, President,
Morehouse College,
Atlanta, Georgia.

Dear Dr. Mays:

Mrs. Marsh received your letter of October 15, but did not have the opportunity to answer it before she left town today on a trip to Savannah and other Georgia points. I am, therefore, writing for her as we would not wish you to think that your letter was being ignored.

I am also going to request you to see me about the matter which you wished to discuss with her. You can understand that Mrs. Marsh has scarcely been able to call her time her own since the publication of her novel. The demands on her time are not as heavy now as they were a few years ago, but the public interest in her book continues and she is still kept very busy. Throughout this period I have attempted to help her in meeting her difficult situation, and to relieve her of part of her burden by handling such engagements as I could.

If you care to discuss the matter with me, I will be glad to have you telephone me in order that we may arrange for an engagement.

Yours very truly,

John R. Marsh

October 22, 1941

Mr. John R. Marsh
463 Electric Building
Atlanta, Georgia

Dear Mr. Marsh:

Your letter to President Mays has been received during his absence from the city. It will be brought to his attention when he returns.

I am sure that he will appreciate your kindness in suggesting an appointment.

Sincerely yours,

M. L. Bunch
Secretary to the President

MLB

November 11, 1941

Mr. John R. Marsh
463 Electric Building
Atlanta, Georgia

Dear Mr. Marsh:

I have been away almost ever since I talked with you some days ago. This letter comes to thank you for the conference and for the usual sympathy and interest which you manifest in what we are trying to do here at Morehouse College.

Although I can understand exactly Mrs. Marsh's situation, I can but hope that she will see her way clear to do something for Morehouse. I am writing her a brief note to this effect.

Thanking you and with kindest regards, I am

Sincerely yours,

Benjamin E. Mays
President

BEM:JEJ

November 11, 1941

Mrs. John R. Marsh
463 Electric Building
Atlanta, Georgia

Dear Mrs. Marsh:

I want to express my appreciation to you for the conference which I had with Mr. Marsh concerning Morehouse College. I hope that you have had time to read the material and listen to our story as related to Mr. Marsh.

I can understand the many demands made upon you for contributions and I can also understand that you have been giving to projects where the needs are obviously urgent. Despite that, <u>please consider us seriously and if you can give us a lift at this time we will be more than grateful</u>.

With kindest regards and best wishes, I am

Sincerely yours,

Benjamin E. Mays

N.B. Would you be willing to speak to our men some time during the school year? We would love to have you come.
B.E.M.

November 11, 1941

Dr. Benjamin E. Mays
Morehouse College
Atlanta, Georgia

Dear Dr. Mays:

Your letter of November 11th to Mrs. Marsh reached us just before we left town on a trip. Mrs. Marsh is still out of the city and I am writing for her.

Whether or not she may consider a donation to Morehouse College I am unable to say, but I cannot offer much encouragement as her list of contributions and donations for 1941 was made up some time ago. My particular reason for writing is to give you an answer to your invitation to Mrs. Marsh to address your students. She appreciates the invitation but she will not be able to accept. She is not a speech-maker and never has been, and she has consistently declined the invitations to make speeches which have come to her since 1936. She does not agree with the current belief that writing a novel or inventing a mouse trap automatically endows a person with oratorical ability. She did not make speeches before her novel was published and she does not feel that she has become qualified to make speeches just because the novel <u>was</u> published. Nevertheless, she thanks you for the invitation and we both send you our good wishes.

Sincerely yours,

John R. Marsh

November 24, 1941

Mr. John R. Marsh
1268 Piedmont Avenue, N.E.
Atlanta, Georgia

Dear Mr. Marsh:

I thank you for your letter of November 11 which was on my desk when I returned to the office this morning. I appreciate all that you say in your letter concerning Mrs. Marsh. I can understand her feeling about speech making. I think it is a most admirable attitude for her to take and yet I know it is difficult to convince the public of that fact.

I also understand the many demands or requests for donations. I can only say that Morehouse College is worthy of her help, that the College has existed here in the heart of the South for seventy-five years and that we feel that the Atlanta public should give its endorsement to and its recognition of an institution which for seventy-five years has served the Negro race and through that the South.

If she can help, I will appreciate it graciously. With kindest regards and best wishes, I am

Sincerely yours,

Benjamin E. Mays
President

BEM:MLB

SEASONS GREETINGS

Man may never abolish war. Man may never get rid of greed and selfishness. He may never eliminate class distinctions and the domination of the weak by the strong. He may never achieve the Good Life. But one fact stands firm -- if he ever achieves the Good Life; if he ever builds a decent world, he will build it on the precepts and examples of a Palestinean Jew who was born in a manger and who died on a cross. The hope of mankind, now as always, is the Star of Bethlehem.

President and Mrs. Benjamin E. Mays
Morehouse College
Atlanta, Georgia

June 22, 1942

Mrs. John R. Marsh
1268 Piedmont Avenue, N.E.
Atlanta, Georgia

Dear Mrs. Marsh:

You recall that last year I wrote you requesting that you help Morehouse College in connection with its $400,000 endowment drive. I had a very pleasant conference with Mr. Marsh. He made it clear that the demands upon you were exceedingly heavy and it would not be possible for you to give any large sum. I am writing now in a slightly different vein.

We have an enrollment of between three-hundred-fifty and four-hundred men. Up to last year we had money for only one scholarship of $40. The coming year we will have approximately $440. I do not mean to say that we do not give any scholarships. We do but when we do we simply do not collect the money. We give scholarships without having money to back them up. Now the college has reached the point where we can not continue to do this.

In the light of the fact mentioned above I am wondering if you would give one tuition scholarship of $80. The hope would be that you would continue to do this each year as long as you are financially able to do so. Please let me hear from you and I hope favorably on this request.

With kindest regards and best wishes, I am

Sincerely yours,

Benjamin E. Mays
President

BEM:JEJ

Mays, President Benjamin E.
Morehouse College
Atlanta

Atlanta, Georgia
June 29, 1942

Dear President Mays:

I have received your letter of June 22nd, requesting that I give a tuition scholarship of $80 to Morehouse College and that I consider making this an annual donation. I am enclosing a check for $80 and I hope it will be of assistance to some fine and deserving student. I am sorry that I cannot promise to make this an annual contribution. The uncertainty of the future based on the war as well as the heavy demands upon me make it impossible for me to promise to do any more.

Whenever I have made any donation to any cause or organization, I have done so with the understanding that no publicity of any type would be given to my contribution. I am sure you understand the reasons behind this and I hope you will keep this matter confidential.

Sincerely,

(Margaret Mitchell)

Mrs. John R. Marsh

July 8, 1942

Mrs. John R. Marsh
1268 Piedmont Avenue, N.E.
Atlanta, Georgia

Dear Mrs. Marsh:

President Mays is out of his office for several days and in his absence I am writing to acknowledge receipt of your letter and contribution to the scholarship fund.

It was indeed kind of you to give a scholarship of $80, receipt for which is enclosed. We appreciate this very much, particularly in light of the fact that so many requests are made of you.

We shall respect your wish not to give publicity to your gift.

Sincerely yours,

(M. L. Bunch)
Secretary to the President

BEM

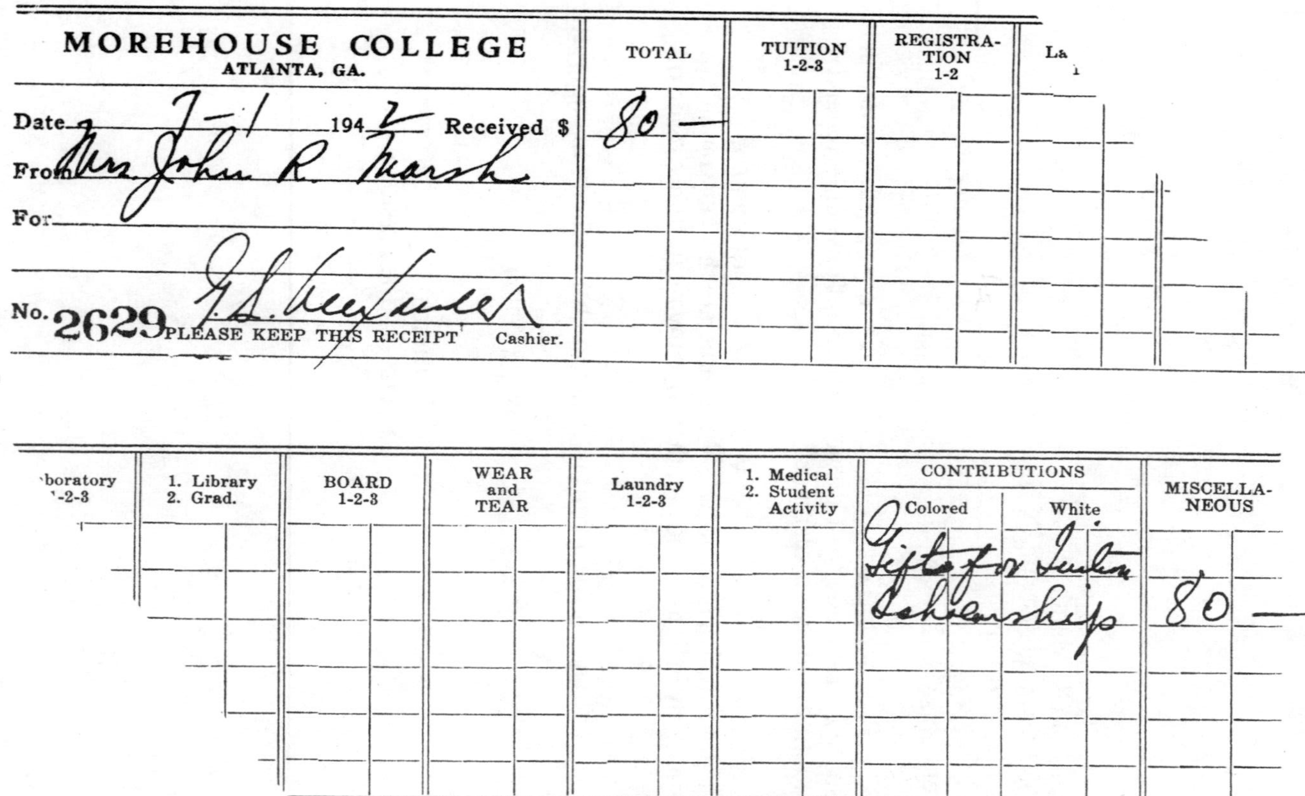

MOREHOUSE COLLEGE
ATLANTA, GA.

Date 7-1 194 2 Received $ 80—
From Mrs. John R. Marsh
For
No. 2629 PLEASE KEEP THIS RECEIPT G. L. Weeks Cashier.

TOTAL	TUITION 1-2-3	REGISTRATION 1-2	La[boratory] 1-2-3
80—			

Laboratory 1-2-3	1. Library 2. Grad.	BOARD 1-2-3	WEAR and TEAR	Laundry 1-2-3	1. Medical 2. Student Activity	CONTRIBUTIONS Colored	CONTRIBUTIONS White	MISCELLANEOUS
						Gift for Tuition Scholarship		80—

July 15, 1942

Mrs. John R. Marsh
1268 Piedmont Avenue, N.E.
Atlanta, Georgia

Dear Mrs. Marsh:

Although my secretary wrote you on July 8 expressing appreciation for your tuition scholarship of $80 to be utilized this coming academic year by some worthy boy, I cannot resist the opportunity to write you myself to express my own personal gratitude for this kind of interest which you are manifesting in what we are doing here. You may rest assured that we shall not give any kind of publicity to this gift.

Although you are quite busy, I hope sometime during the next school year it will be possible for you and Mr. Marsh to come out to Morehouse College to see in detail what is happening here. I feel that so many of our leading citizens have not had the privilege of seeing Morehouse and the affiliated institutions, although the schools have been here for many, many years.

I appreciate your gift all the more when I know that the appeals that come to you must be multitudinous.

Again thanking you and with kindest regards, I am

Sincerely yours,

Benjamin E. Mays
President

BEM:MLB

May 10, 1943

Dear Mrs. Marsh:

We have just held an annual meeting of the Board of Trustees of Morehouse College, and the members of the Board want me to express our appreciation to you for your scholarship contribution. It helped us in two ways:

1. It enabled the college to award a scholarship of $80 to Charles W. King, a young man deserving help who would have had a very difficult time making it through the year without your aid. He did very good work - averaging 3.80, which is an A minus average.

2. Despite the drainage of close to 200 men to the armed forces from September to now, and certainly the number by June 1, we shall close the year out of the red. You helped make this possible, and we are grateful.

We began September with 400 men and we will close June 1 with about 200. Since we are a college for men only, next year will be much worse for us, but we plan to carry on and we have faith enough to believe that we will win through. At any rate, we face the future unafraid.

Appreciating your interest in the work, and with kindest regards, I am

Yours sincerely,

Benjamin E. Mays
President

BEM:G

Mrs. John R. Marsh
1268 Piedmont Avenue, N.E.
Atlanta, Georgia

Mays, President Benjamin E.
Morehouse College, S.W.
Atlanta

Atlanta, Georgia
May 24, 1943

My dear President Mays:

I was glad to have your letter telling me of the excellent record of Charles W. King. I am glad that my donation went toward helping him through this past year at college. I am enclosing a check for eighty dollars, to be awarded to the student you and the Board of Trustees feel to be most deserving of aid in this coming year. If you decide upon Charles King again, that certainly has my approval; but if he has finished college or if you feel that there is some other student who needs it more, please use your own judgment.

I know what the war is doing to colleges all over the country, and so my congratulations go to you for finishing this difficult year "out of the red."

Sincerely,

(Margaret Mitchell)

Mrs. John R. Marsh

May 28, 1943

Dear Mrs. Marsh:

This letter comes to express my deep appreciation to you for your letter of May 24 enclosing a check for $80 to be used as a scholarship for Charles King for next year or for some other worthy student.

We were able to get around twenty-five scholarships because people in different parts of the country were kind enough to do what you did. I understand that you do not wish to have this publicized and I assure you that it will not be.

I am still hoping that at some time convenient to you it will be possible for you to come out to Morehouse and see this set up here. We have, as you know five institutions in close proximity to each other doing a coooperative job that cannot be surpassed anywhere in the United States. I think what we are doing would please you.

Of course, Morehouse being an institution for men only will be greatly hit next year. We began last year in September with 400 men but by June 1 of this year all of those men will be 18 years old and above except 31. We are attempting now to recruit students 16 and 17 years old for our enrollment in the fall. The financial situation will be precarious for us, but I am quite sure that an institution that has served Georgia for 75 years will not suffer unduly because its men go to war to help make the world safe for democracy.

Again thanking you for your kindness, and with kindest regards, I am

Yours sincerely,

Benjamin E. Mays
President

Mrs. John R. Marsh
1268 Piedmont
Atlanta, Georgia

June 4, 1943

Dear Mrs. Marsh:

In my letter to you a few days ago I did not send you an official receipt for the $80 scholarship contribution, which you were kind enough to send to us. I am sending the receipt in this mail.

Again thanking you, and with best wishes, I am

Yours sincerely,

Benjamin E. Mays
President

BEM:G
Encl.

Mrs. John R. Marsh
1268 Piedmont N E
Atlanta
Georgia

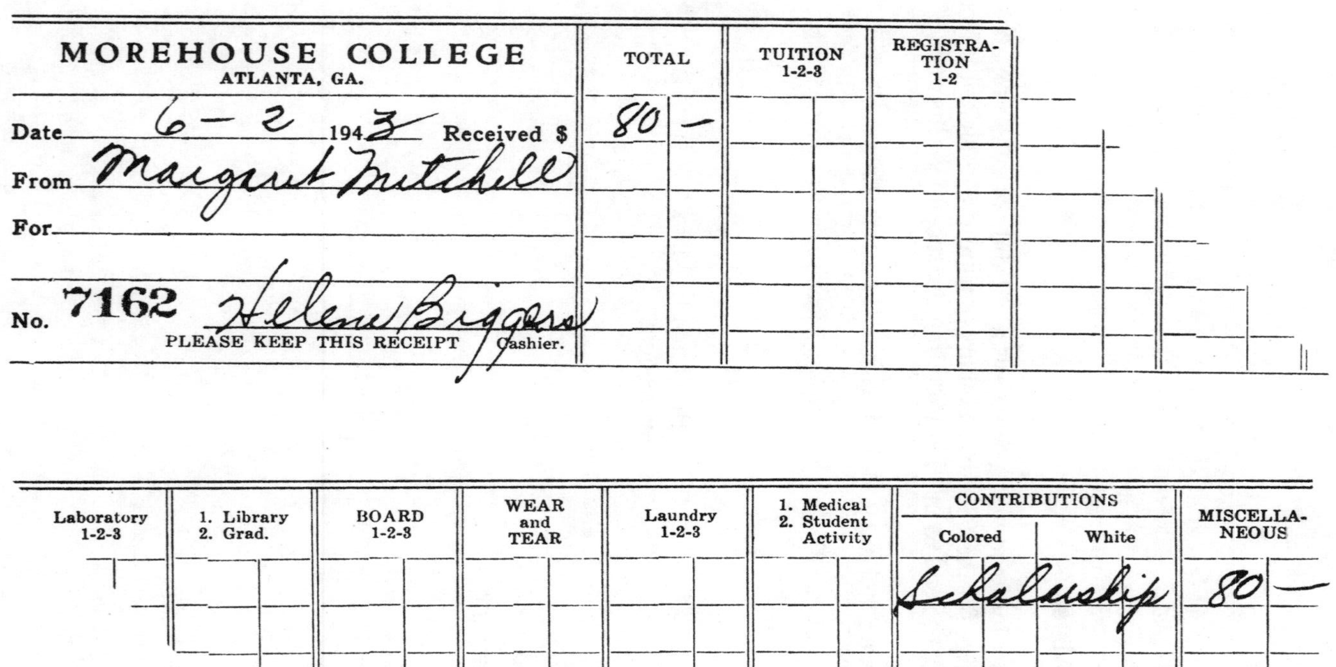

MOREHOUSE COLLEGE
ATLANTA, GA.

Date 6-2 1943 Received $
From Margaret Mitchell
For
No. 7162 Helene Biggers Cashier.
PLEASE KEEP THIS RECEIPT

TOTAL	TUITION 1-2-3	REGISTRATION 1-2
80—		

Laboratory 1-2-3	1. Library 2. Grad.	BOARD 1-2-3	WEAR and TEAR	Laundry 1-2-3	1. Medical 2. Student Activity	CONTRIBUTIONS Colored	CONTRIBUTIONS White	MISCELLANEOUS
						Scholarship		80—

July 6, 1944

Dear Mrs. Marsh:

You and friends like you made it possible for Morehouse to come through the past year in good condition. We closed June 30, 1944 out of the red - books balanced. Without the warm response from graduates and friends of the College, the War would have crippled Morehouse months ago. You helped so that this did not happen. We are thankful and obligated to you for your generous assistance.

The unfortunate thing about our situation is the fact that we must repeat this year, July 1944 through June 30, 1945, what we did during the year that closed June 30. In order to get the College through this year, we must raise for the current budget $25,270, which is only $730 less than we set out to raise last year. If the persons who gave scholarships last year will give the same amount this year and give it about the same time they gave last year, we will close June 30, 1945 in good shape again. Your contribution was made in July 1943.

Then too, if we can get the current budget for this year underwritten, guaranteed, the president of the College will be free to spend the whole of this year raising $330,000 on endowment which amount must be secured before June 30, 1945 in order to get the General Education Board to give an equal amount in which case the endowment would be increased by $660,000.

This letter comes, therefore, to request you to contribute to Morehouse this year, which began July 1, 1944, at least as much as you contributed last year. For your convenience, I am enclosing a card for you to sign and return.

Thanking you for your help in the past and soliciting your continued interest and help in the future, I am

Sincerely yours,
Benjamin E. Mays
President

Mrs. John R. Marsh
1268 Piedmont Avenue, N.E., Atlanta, Georgia

N.B. I still want you to see Morehouse. I hope you will come out sometime. B.E.M.

Mays, President Benjamin E.
Morehouse College
Atlanta

Atlanta, Georgia
July 18, 1944

My dear President Mays:

I am enclosing a check for $100.00, which I hope you will use to help some deserving student through the coming year.

Sincerely,

(Margaret Mitchell)

Mrs. John R. Marsh

July 20, 1944

Mrs. Margaret Mitchell Marsh
1268 Piedmont Avenue, N.E., Apt. 3
Atlanta, Georgia

Dear Mrs. Marsh:

I am certainly grateful to you for your continued interest in Morehouse College. I appreciate your interest and your contribution more than you can know. I am enclosing an official receipt.

With kindest regards and best wishes, I am

Yours truly,

Benjamin E. Mays
President

BEM:B
Encl.

Atlanta, April 17, 1946

Dear Hughes
(Hughes Spalding, Sr., Chair, Fulton DeKalb Hospital Authority):

Thank you for the invitation to attend the dinner on April 24 to discuss the need for greater hospital facilities in Atlanta and plans for expansion of St. Joseph's Infirmary. I'm sorry I can't be with you. John is still in bed and I do not feel easy about leaving him. He is not in any acutely serious condition but I would feel nervous if I left him alone at night. I haven't been anywhere except to the grocery since he got out of the hospital.

I'm very interested in better hospital facilities in Atlanta, especially for colored people. Recently our colored laundress, who worked for us for over twenty years, died of cancer. She was failing at the time I brought John home from the Brunswick hospital. I discovered that Steiner had been kindness itself and had done all they could do, her private physician had done his best. Her family are self-respecting people who have always paid their way and they were anxious to do all they could to ease Carrie. It fell upon me to find a hospital bed in which Carrie could die more comfortably than at home. I do not want ever again to go through the agonizing experiences I had. There just were no beds. It was not that Carrie's family and I were unwilling to pay. Carrie was like my own family and I would have paid all that I would have paid for a relative. The best promise we could get was a hospital bed in two or three weeks at Harris Memorial. We hoped Carrie would not last two or three weeks.

Finally I bethought myself of the Sisters of Our Lady of Perpetual Help and I threw myself upon them. I do not know if they violated their rule that their patients must be friendless and without money. At any rate, they took Carrie in and cared for her until she died three days later. It was with great gratitude that I made a donation to them.

I do not think people who have not experienced so heartbreaking a time can realize the need for more beds for our colored population who are able to pay something for medical and hospital care. I hope so much that some thought will be taken of this particular problem. We have heard so often in the past twenty years discussions of the problems of medical care for the white-collar class who are not rich enough for the $9 a day at a hospital but who make enough money to keep them out of charity wards. Atlanta is big enough now to have colored people in the white-collar class, and I wonder how many of them have been in the situation of our Carrie, willing to pay but being unable to buy a bed in which to die.

The foregoing does not mean a lack of interest in hospital facilities for white people. I am interested and I hope to hear wonderful things. It is just that I feel many people are aware of the need for helping white people but most people are unaware of the Negro problem and are apt to dismiss it by saying "why don't they go to Grady?"

I am enclosing a check for $1,000 as a gift from John and me to the St. Joseph's Building Fund. My mother and my father both experienced the kind care of the sisters at the Infirmary. As you perhaps know, they both died at St. Joseph's and John and I are giving this in their memory.

More power to your meeting and your work.

(Margaret Mitchell)
Mrs John R. Marsh

May 8, 1946

Mrs. John R. Marsh
1268 Piedmont Avenue, Northeast
Atlanta, Georgia

Dear Mrs. Marsh:

It was indeed satisfying to know that there is the possibility of your establishing a Memorial Fund at Morehouse College which will be used to further medical education among Negroes. Morehouse, for many years now, has been strong in its pre-medical and pre-dental work, thus enabling our students to enter first-class medical schools without being handicapped.

Although I do not know how you plan to handle the Fund, I feel that I should discuss cost so that you may get some idea of the situation here at Morehouse College and elsewhere. Excluding laboratory fees and books, it cost approximately $446 per year to attend Morehouse College. The breakdown is as follows:

Tuition ----------------	$130	
Fees ------------------	28	
Room, Board, Laundry-	288	as of September 1, 1946
Total Cost	$446 per year	

Excluding laboratory fees and books, the cost is $158 per year for Atlanta students who live at home.

If you desire to establish scholarships to cover tuition only for several students that is one thing; but another if you plan scholarships to cover the total cost for the student. If the former it would be $130 per student and $446 per student for the latter. I am assuming that you would want to establish something that would be permanent rather than something that would have to be paid from capital funds each year.

I wish you would consider endowing the scholarships. For example, $10,000 invested might yield 3%, thus guaranteeing $300 a year; $5,000 would guarantee a scholarship of $150 per year; $25,000 would guarantee $750 per year. On the basis of a $130 scholarship, several would be helped on the largest sum, two on the middle sum, and one on the smallest sum. If you give it as endowment to be used as stipulated above, we could get it matched dollar for dollar by the General Education Board: a $5,000 contribution would be matched by $5,000, thus making $10,000. And I am sure that if several scholarships were involved, the income on the total amount could be used for scholarships.

The two medical schools in America established mainly for negroes are Howard University and Meharry Medical School. Meharry is located in Nashville, Tennessee and Howard is located in Washington, D. C. Tuition at Meharry is $300 per year for three quarters, other fees amount to $45.50. Books are estimated at $60, making a total of $405.50, excluding room and board. At least another $300 would have to be added for that item, making the annual cost not less than $700. There are many other items that a medical student must have, such as microscopes and the like; so I am of the opinion, that it would cost the student close to $900 to do his medical work at Meharry.

Tuition at Howard University amounts to approximately $275. This does not incude books and other special fees. Room and board are around $315 per year. The Howard catalog does not give as much of a breakdown as Meharry, but I am of the opinion that the cost at Howard would be easily $800 or $900 a year. These fees are taken from a catalog two or three years old and it is conceivable that the fees are slightly higher than this now. I am also stating below the fees in one of the medical schools primarily established for whites.

Matriculation Fee ---	$	5.00	
Tuition -------------		221.50	(State residents)
Tuition -------------		426.50	(Out of State residents)
Breakage Deposit ---		25.00	
Microscope fee -----		10.00	
Total ---------------	$	466.00	for Out of State residents

The above fees were taken from the Indiana University catalog.

Although I know that you are exceedingly busy at this time, and are being confined because of Mr. Marsh's condition, I would be very happy to come out one day next week, at a time convenient to you, and talk the matter over with you further. I wish you would consider the possibility of giving more latitude as to where the recipient of the scholarship ought to practice. Any part of the south may be just as much in need as Georgia or Atlanta.

With kindest regards and best wishes to you, I am

Yours truly,

Benjamin E. Mays
President

BEM:ch

N.B. The cost at Indiana University does not include room and board, which will probably be another $400.

May 14, 1946

Mrs. John R. Marsh
1268 Piedmont Avenue, Northeast
Atlanta, Georgia

Dear Mrs. Marsh:

I am sending you in this mail a booklet of mine just off the press under the caption, Seeking To Be Christian in Race Relations. It is brief and can be read easily in two hours or less. I hope you will find it good reading.

With kindest regards and best wishes, I am

Yours truly,

Benjamin E. Mays
President

BEM:ch

N.B. Thanks for your message. I am in town until Thursday of next week. Hope Mr. Marsh improves.

B.E.M.

Wed, PM, 5/22/46

Woman called for Dr. Mays of Morehouse to inquire about John. I explained that John's being worse since last Saturday was reason why you had not phoned. & I said you wouldn't be able to communicate with Dr. Mays by Thursday (when he is going out of town). He will be away only for week-end.

Mays, Dr. Benjamin E.
Morehouse College
Atlanta, Ga.

Atlanta, Georgia
July 5, 1946

My dear President Mays:

I am sorrier than I can tell you that circumstances have prevented the meeting for discussion of money for a scholarship for one of your students. I am embarrassed that I have not even been able to talk with you over the phone -- when I phoned, you were out; when you phoned I was out or my husband's condition was such that I could not leave him. He is better now but his illness is such that he has many setbacks, and so I can never count on my time from one hour to the next. I have had to give up any idea of attending to anything except his illness. I hope that he is on the road to recovery now and that some time soon we can have the discussion I mentioned over the phone to you. It just is not possible now. I have not even had the opportunity to talk matters over with the Trust Company of Georgia who assist and advise me in such affairs, and I do not know when I will have the opportunity to talk with them.

I realize now that I was premature in thinking that my husband's condition had improved to such a point that I could again take up things in my outside life once more. I hope you will understand my situation and that I will have to postpone this matter until later.

Cordially,

(Margaret Mitchell Marsh)

Mrs. John R. Marsh

July 8, 1946

Mrs. Margaret Mitchell Marsh
1268 Piedmont Avenue, N.E.
Atlanta, Georgia

Dear Mrs. Marsh:

I thank you for your letter of July 5th. I am very sorry to learn that Mr. Marsh's condition does not improve as positively and as rapidly as we all hope. I can understand with deep sympathy the situation through which you are now passing. I am hoping with you that things will be better for Mr. Marsh.

I think it would be wise for me to wait now several weeks before contacting you again. In the meantime, if you see your way clear to talk with me further before two or three months, I would appreciate it if you would telephone me or write me.

Again thanking you for your letter and wishing the best of everything for you and for Mr. Marsh, I am

Yours truly,

Benjamin E. Mays
President

BEM:B

Atlanta 5, Georgia
October 23, 1946

My dear President Mays:

I have not forgotten about the matter we discussed last spring by mail. I have thought so often that the time would come when I could have a conversation with you either in person or over the phone. My husband's illness has continued. At last I believe I see enough improvement in his condition to warrant feeling that he is on the road to recovery. Still, he has not recovered enough for me to call any of my time my own. So, instead of having the pleasure of discussing the matter of assisting in the dental and medical education of Negro students, I will just have to send you a check and ask you to arrange matters.

As I believe I told you, I wish to aid medical and dental students in honor of the memory of a Negro friend, Carrie Mitchell Holbrook, who died last spring. One of her nephews, Grady Bennett, junior, is a student at Morehouse. It is his wish to be a doctor and it was his aunt's wish too. Years ago we promised Carrie that we would see to it that Grady was assisted in getting the best medical education possible. As I understand it, the GI Bill of Rights arranges things for Grady's tuition at Morehouse. And I have made arrangements for his tuition at Meharry or any other good medical college he may choose. I am enclosing the legal paper; which explains this, because you are named in it. I hope it meets with your approval. I had to get up the paper so speedily in an interval of my husband's illness that there was no time to consult you. You will note that should anything happen to prevent Grady Bennett, junior, from going to medical school, this sum ($3,000) shall revert to you or your successor in office as President of Morehouse, to be expended for medical and dental education of your students. I sincerely hope that nothing prevents Grady from receiving a medical education, but if something should arise to make it impossible then the disposition of this $3,000 is at the discretion of you or your successor.

Life being uncertain at best, I put this matter into the hands of the Trust Officer of the Citizens and Southern National

Bank, so that in the event of my death or a long absence from the city or even the country, Grady's medical education would be taken care of. I asked Grady to discuss this matter with you, as I did not know when the time would come when I would have the opportunity to do so.

And now, about this check for $2,000 which I am enclosing -- it also is given in memory of Carrie Holbrook. I want it used to assist deserving students in acquiring medical and dental education. I think I may speak for Carrie, as well as for myself, when I say that both of us would prefer the students to be chosen on a basis of character, good will toward their fellow man, and willingness to work, rather than on brilliance or high scholastic grades alone. In the beginning it was my wish that you use this money to assist through medical school some of your students who already had their Morehouse tuition paid under the G.I. Bill or through scholarships. It seemed to me at that time a good idea to assist a student who had already finished his pre-medical work. Now, however, I must leave that to your judgment. You may use this in assisting one student through medical school, or several; you may use it for one student or several students at Morehouse so that they can finish their pre-medical there; if you think it best to have it matched by the General Education Board, I am agreeable to this too, and this letter is your authority to take up the matter with the General Education Board.

You will recall that the only stipulation I made was that the young men should practice in Georgia or Atlanta, and you took issue with me on that subject, stating, with truth, that "any part of the South may be just as much in need as Georgia or Atlanta." I realize the truth of what you said. Unfortunately, however, I see the desperate need in Atlanta and in Georgia. I believe I know this need more than the average white person not in social service work. I want to better my own state and my own section. I do not doubt that other states have equally desperate needs but I feel that each state and each section should take care of its own. Georgia is a huge state and is poor. We are poorer in Negro doctors, I am sure, than almost any other state. Therefore, I would definitely prefer that any boys who avail themselves of this money should practice in Georgia or at least give Georgia a trial of a year or so.

It is very disheartening to those who try to do something for the upbuilding of their state and section to see the smartest brains drained off from the South to crowded Northern sections. When one has paid taxes, given money, sided and encouraged whites and Negroes to make better people of themselves and a better state, it is discouraging to have them leave this section. The time will come when Atlanta will be the largest Negro city in the south, the time will come when we will have a large and, I hope, famous Negro hospital for training boys and girls from this section. When that time comes, I hope we will have enough excellent Negro doctors in this section to staff this hospital.

Still, if circumstances indicate that practice in some other Southern state is necessary for the livelihood or happiness of some young Negro doctor, I would hate to feel that I had stood in the way. So I must leave that to your discretion too, but I ask that you make very clear to anyone who accepts this money for medical or dental training that it would be the wish of Carrie Mitchell Holbrook that they stay here and help their own people.

I have made out this check to you. If this is not the correct way to do it, please let me know, return the check, and I will fill it out in the manner you direct.

Cordially,

Margaret Mitchell Marsh

(Mrs. John R. Marsh)

October 23, 1946

Mrs. John R. Marsh
1268 Piedmont Avenue, Northeast
Atlanta, Georgia

Dear Mrs. Marsh:

Your letter addressed to President Mays arrived during his absence from the city. He will return to the office on Tuesday and your letter will be brought to his attention at that time.

Sincerely,

(Cordelia M. Hill)

Secretary to Dr. Mays

h

November 1, 1946

Mrs. John R. Marsh
1268 Piedmont Avenue, Northeast
Atlanta, Georgia

Dear Mrs. Marsh:

I thank you more than you know for your letter of October 23 and for the check for $2,000. Most of all I am pleased to know that Mr. Marsh is improving. I hope that he will recover completely within the very near future.

I was deeply moved by your letter and impressed with it beyond words. You show deep understanding and a grasp of the total problem. It was a pleasure to read your letter and to see the deep interest which you have in our common problem. I am still hoping that it will be possible for you to come out and address our students at a time convenient to you.

Whatever disposition we finally make of the $2,000, it must be acceptable to you. Right now I am inclined to feel that it should be used as endowment and the income on that amount should go to some student looking forward to a medical career. We could choose one boy and help him for four years here at Morehouse and help him for four years in Medical School. That being true, we will be able to get a new man every eighth year. Or if you prefer, we could help a man who graduates from Morehouse and give him the income on the $2,000 over a period of four years while he is in Medical School. I grant you that this will be only about $80, but it would be continuous for four years and at the same time it would help Negro students for an indefinite period of time. In fact, we will be doing something for them for many years to come.

If you feel that the approximate $80 on the income would be too small to be of real value to a student, we would be willing to use the $2,000 which the General Education Board will match and then have an income on $4,000. This would amount to approximately

$160 a year if we could get 4%. In this case, we could help one boy in Medical School for four years, giving him approximately $160 per year. This would be an appreciable lift. I believe this would be better than helping two boys by giving them $1,000 each or one boy by giving him $2,000. Then your work and that of Mrs. Holbrook would live on indefinitely. Please let me know about this.

With kindest regards and best wishes, I am

Yours truly,

Benjamin E. Mays
President

BEM:ch
Encl

N.B. *Whenever you think you can afford it, I would like for us to discuss all phases of this subject. I thank you too for sending a copy of the arrangements made for the medical education of Grady Bennett.*

B.E.M.

Atlanta 5, Georgia

November 7, 1946

Dear President Mays:

Thank you for giving me your ideas on the best use to be made of the $2,000 I sent you for medical and dental students. I believe it would be more sensible to match this $2,000 with the $2,000 the General Education Board will give. One hundred and sixty dollars a year would be some help to a boy taking a medical degree and, with the rising cost of living now, $80 would not go very far. I'll be glad to know how it works out and I'll leave the details to you.

Cordially,

(Margaret Mitchell Marsh)

Mrs. John Marsh

November 13, 1946

Mrs. Margaret Mitchell Marsh
1268 Piedmont Avenue, Northeast
Atlanta, Georgia

Dear Mrs. Marsh:

I thank you for your letter of November 7. I am glad you like the suggestion of having the General Education Board match the $2,000 which you contributed recently. I shall work out details and will be communicating with you again within the next several days. It may be two or three weeks before I can get to it.

Again thanking you and with kindest regards and best wishes always, I am

Yours truly,

Benjamin E. Mays
President

BEM:ch

N.B. I hope Mr. Marsh continues to improve.

B.E.M.

March 14, 1947

Mrs. John Marsh
1268 Piedmont Avenue, N.E.
Atlanta, Georgia

Dear Mrs. Marsh:

I am writing good news to friends of Morehouse who have stood by us since I came to the college as its president in July of 1940.

The $400,000 which we had to raise in 1940 has been reduced to $50,000. Of the $50,000 yet to be raised about $23,000 is pledged, leaving only $27,000 in new money to be secured. To state it another way, the Morehouse endowment has been increased by approximately $700,000. You see the General Education Board has been matching what we raised dollar for dollar. They will match $50,000 more. For all purposes, we have raised close to $800,000 in six and one-half years. We are obligated to you for your support and friendship in the past and we cherish both for the days ahead.

We will soon be ready to turn our hands to other needs such as buildings while at the same time we will be working to increase the endowment up to the $2,000,000 mark. Experts say that a college the size of Morehouse needs an endowment of $3,000,000.

It will probably be four months before I write you again because by agreement the college that participates in the United Negro College Fund must devote all of their time and energy to the United effort from March 15 through July 15.

We will inform you in the late summer and early fall of the college's achievements along all lines. Again thanking you for all you have done for Morehouse and with kindest regards and best wishes, I am

Yours truly,
Benjamin E. Mays
President

(Dictated: March 12, 1947)

May 28, 1947

Mrs. John Marsh
1268 Piedmont Avenue, N.E.
Atlanta, Georgia

Dear Mrs. Marsh:

I am enclosing a copy of the statement to be carried in the next issue of the Morehouse catalog relative to the Carrie Mitchell Holbrook Memorial Fund. Please let me know if this statement meets with your approval.

With kindest regards and best wishes, I am

Yours truly,

Benjamin E. Mays
President

BEM:ch
Encl

N.B. *Mr. Marsh liked it but we can catch errors or make minor changes when we receive the proof.*

B.E.M.

The Carrie Mitchell Holbrook Memorial Fund

Mrs. Margaret Mitchell Marsh of Atlanta, Georgia contributed in November 1946 $2,000 to the Morehouse endowment fund in memory of Mrs. Carrie Mitchell Holbrook. The $2,000 contributed by Mrs. Marsh has been matched by the General Education Board. The income of the full amount of $4,000 is to be used for scholarship aid for a worthy Morehouse graduate of high scholarship who is studying medicine with the view of practicing in Georgia or in some other southern state. The student who will practice in Georgia will have first claim always on the scholarship grant.

(November 1, 1946)

November 9, 1948

Mrs. John Marsh
1268 Piedmont Avenue, NE
Atlanta, Georgia

Dear Mrs. Marsh:

With your financial and moral support, the Morehouse endowment has been increased approximately $1,000,000 during the past eight years. It could not have been done without you and friends like you. Our endowment is now $2,000,000.

Although the endowment for Morehouse should be $3,000,000, we must turn now to the physical plant. Very soon we will launch a campaign for a chemistry building, to be used by four colleges and the university, a gynmasium, two dormitories, and a chapel. When the campaign is launched, we will need your continued interest and support. To do the next job, we will need the friends we have and we will need to cultivate new friends.

We are off to a good start this year. We have 771 men enrolled from 33 states. The faculty is good and the morale is high.

With kindest regards and best wishes to you, I am

Sincerely yours,

Benjamin E. Mays
President

BEM:dem

March 12, 1949

Mr. and Mrs. John Marsh
1268 Piedmont Avenue, NE
Atlanta,
Georgia

Dear Mr. and Mrs. Marsh:

This letter comes to inform you that we will not be able to work further on the $3,000,000 campaign for Morehouse College until after July 15. Beginning March 15 and extending through July 15, the thirty-two member colleges can work only in the interest of the United Negro College Fund.

In the early Fall we hope to have the $3,000,000 campaign definitely on its way and we covet your continued interest and good will as we move forward in the biggest financial effort ever launched in the interest of Morehouse College. We can not afford to lose the interest of a single person and I hope that you will be with us in the future as you have been in the past.

We had on hand on Founder's Day, February 18, around $7,000. So our efforts are already beginning to bear fruit.

In this new effort we are trying to secure the maximum participation and contributions from our alumni. I thought you would be interested in this special appeal to our graduates.

With kindest regards and best wishes, I am

Yours truly,

Benjamin E. Mays
President

BEM:dem

(Reprinted from)

THE
Pittsburgh Courier

SATURDAY, SEPT. 10, 1949

Miss Mitchell's Death is Due to the South's General Leniency With Law's White Violators

== By BENJAMIN E. MAYS ==

(The views expressed in this column are those of the writer and do not necessarily express the editorial opinion of the Pittsburgh Courier. -- The Editors.)

Margaret Mitchell, author of "Gone With the Wind," died at noon, Tuesday, Aug. 18. Five days before, she had been struck down by an automobile and she never fully regained consciousness. The world waited and prayed, hoping that Miss Mitchell (Mrs. John Marsh) would soon recover.

The telegrams, letters, telephone calls came from everywhere. But she was too badly injured to recover. Everybody was pulling for her and no one wanted Margaret Mitchell to die. It was partly because she was a famous person. But it was also due to the fact that Margaret Mitchell was loved by millions of people.

She was simple and modest. Her fame and popularity did not go to her head. The people who knew her intimately loved her dearly. Those who knew her only from her book, "Gone With The Wind." admired her with deep affection. She wore her fame as a loose garment, and that can be said of only a few people who achieve fame. She is perhaps the greatest author the South has produced and one of the world's great authors.

THERE IS SOMETHING tragic in her death. She had no right to die the way she did. It seems that the driver of the car that struck her was speeding and besides, evidence seems to indicate that he had been drinking. These are the reasons why I say she did not have to go that way. But I want to say something else about the driver that struck her.

According to an editorial in the Atlanta Constitution, of August 14, the driver of the car, Hugh D. Gravitt, "had been arrested twenty-four times for traffic violations, many of them serious. The editorial states further that the driver began his record of violations four years ago and the fines grew less.

"He was fined $7 in 1944 for reckless driving." In later years the charges were "suspended" or he was given small fines, one as low as $5.

* * *

NO NEGRO COULD have been arrested twenty-four times for traffic violations. He would not have been allowed to get that many. After a few violations, I believe, the Negro's license would have been permanently revoked. If the law had been as strict for this reckless white driver as it is on reckless Negro drivers, Miss Mitchell would have been living today because Hugh D. Gravitt would not have been driving his taxi or private car which hit Margaret Mitchell.

All this probably means that the law in the South is too hard on Negroes and too easy on white people. To me it seems clear that if Southern law leans over backwards to see that Negroes are punished severely, it will also lean over backward to see to it that white people are not punished severely. But injustice takes its toll in unpredictable places.

The death of Margaret Mitchell, I believe, is due in part to this discriminatory policy of the South. The white man in the South can get away with almost anything. Certainly he can get away with scores of things that a Negro could never get away with. I cannot conceive of any man being arrested twenty-four times for traffic violations and at the same time being permitted to retain his license.

* * *

I AM STILL convinced that it could never be thus with a Negro. The cost of Atlanta's neglect in allowing a man like this to drive is entirely too dear. I would hate for it to be anyone, but it was certainly most unfortunate that it had to be Margaret Mitchell.

But it took the death of a famous person to arouse Atlanta to its duty and sense of responsibility. Something will be done now. Taxi drivers and all drivers will be scrutinized more thoroughly. It's an ill-wind that blows nobody good. If an ordinary citizen had been struck down perhaps the incident would have passed unnoticed.

Certainly, if a Negro had died this way the chances are great that Atlanta would not have been aroused. Be that as it may, I hope this incident will be the means to saving the lives of others and the means of Atlanta and the South being as strict on white people who violate traffic laws as it is on a Negro who violates it.

But nothing that we do now can amend the wrong that has been done. Gravitt's tears and Gravitt's prayers cannot raise Margaret Mitchell from the dead. He may repent and God may forgive him, but Miss Mitchell is gone and hearts will ache and bleed because a reckless driver was given too much freedom.

========================

October 20, 1949

Mr. John Marsh
1266 Piedmont Avenue, NE
Atlanta, Georgia

Dear Mr. Marsh:

I thought you would be interested to receive a word from the college at the very opening of the year. So I am writing a letter to several hundreds of our friends to give them a bit of information about Morehouse.

Despite the fact that our enrollment is slightly below what we had anticipated, Morehouse College has gotten off to an exceptionally good start. We had set a budget for about 660 and we have 610. We are about 50 students short and we will have to revise our budget to obviate a deficit by cutting $12,000 from the approved budget. I believe the adjustment can be made to enable us to close in 1950 without a deficit. This is important because during the nine years of my presidency, we have never had a deficit.

Our expansion campaign is on quietly and it will be perhaps two, three, or four weeks before we make public announcements. The trustees feel that we should get a firm to conduct the campaign and we are held up at that point. As you know the first segment of our campaign calls for $500,000 for a new chemistry building which will serve all of the colleges in the center. I will give more details about this later.

We had to do something immediately about student housing so the five units authorized by the Board of Trustees are nearing completion. We can house 115 men in the five units at the low cost of $112,000 which amount we took from endowment and current funds. These units will take the place of the first temporary dormitory built by the Government for veterans.

Several of our teachers who were studying last year have returned to the college and I am quite convinced that our faculty is stronger than ever before. It is an inspiring group and I feel that we are doing one of the finest jobs to be found anywhere.

As for myself, I returned to the college August 10 after being away for forty-three days in Europe. I went to England first to attend the Central Committee meeting of the World Council of Churches. I was privileged to travel through some other parts of Europe before returning.

Thanking you for your past interest in our work and soliciting your continued prayers and help, I am

Yours truly,

Benjamin E. Mays
President

SPALDING, SIBLLEY, TROUTMAN & KELLEY
434 TRUST COMPANY OF GEORGIA BUILDING
Atlanta 3 Georgia

December 23, 1949

Mr. Stephens Mitchell
Peters Building
Atlanta, Georgia

Dear Steve:

I am happy to say that Fulton-DeKalb Hospital Authority has funds in hand with which to build a pay hospital for negroes at the southeast corner of Butler Street and Coca-Cola Place. The contract for erection of this hospital has been let, and actual work will commence within a few weeks. It is a source of pride that we should be able here in Atlanta and Georgia to build a hospital of this nature in order to look after the needs of members of the negro race who are not eligible at Grady and who therefore have no place to go when ill.

I can frankly say that I was the chief sponsor of this idea for a pay negro hospital and that Frank Wilson and I sold it not only to the trustees of the hospital, but to the Fulton County Medical Society and to all other groups in this community which are interested in social welfare.

However, your sister, Margaret Mitchell Marsh, originated the idea with me, what I mean to say is that until after she discussed it with me, it never occurred to me that it was a step that could be successfully taken.

In the spring of 1946, I requested Margaret to make a contribution to assist in building a new hospital for St. Joseph's Infirmary. She and John very graciously sent me a check for One Thousand ($1,000.00) Dollars to apply towards this good cause. At the same time she wrote me a letter dated April 17, 1946, and in that letter pleaded the cause of a negro hospital of this nature and shortly thereafter I began to work on the project, and after two or three years it is an actuality. I wish to quote you from her letter to me as follows:

> *I'm very interested in better hospital facilities in Atlanta, especially for colored people. Recently our colored laundress, who worked for us for over twenty years, died of cancer. She was failing at the time I brought John home from the Brunswick hospital. I discovered that Steiner had been kindness itself and had done all they could do, her private physician had done his best. Her family are self-respecting people who have always paid their way and they were anxious to do all they could to ease Carrie. It fell upon me to find a hospital bed in which Carrie could die more comfortably than at home. I do not want ever again to go through the agonizing experiences I had. There just were no beds. It was not that Carrie's family and I were unwilling to pay. Carrie was like my own family and I would have paid all that I would have paid for a relative. The best promise we could get was a hospital bed in two or three weeks at Harris Memorial. We hoped Carrie would not last two or three weeks.*
>
> *Finally I bethought myself of the Sisters of Our Lady of Perpetual Help and I threw myself upon them. I do not know if they violated their rule that their patients must be friendless and without money. At any rate, they took Carrie in and cared for her until she died three days*

later. It was with great gratitude that I made a donation to them.

I do not think people who have not experienced so heartbreaking a time can realize the need for more beds for our colored population who are able to pay something for medical and hospital care. I hope so much that some thought will be taken of this particular problem. We have heard so often in ther past twenty years discussions of the problems of medical care for the white-collar class who are not rich enough for the $9 a day at a hospital but who make enough money to keep them out of charity wards. Atlanta is big enough now to have colored people in the white-collar class, and I wonder how many of them have been in the situation of our Carrie, willing to pay but being unable to buy a bed in which to die.

The foregoing does not mean a lack of interest in hospital facilities for white people. I am interested and I hope to hear wonderful things. It is just that I feel many people are aware of the need for helping white people but most people are unaware of the Negro problem and are apt to dismiss it by saying "why don't they go to Grady?"

I feel that you and John will be interested in learning that Margaret was really the motivating influence which brought this pay hospital for negroes to fruition.

Personal wishes.

Very Sincerely,
Hughes Spalding

HS:cw
CC: Mr. John Marsh

1268 Piedmont Avenue, N.E.
Atlanta 5, Georgia

March 27, 1950

Mr. Hughes Spalding
Trust Company of Georgia Building
Atlanta, Georgia

Dear Mr. Spalding:

Here are some additional thoughts I have had regarding the naming of the new Negro hospital the "Margaret Mitchell Marsh Memorial Hospital." I had expected that Steve Mitchell and I would both call on you regarding your letter. So, I had not gotten my ideas rounded out in my own mind when you telephoned me. Here are the additional matters I am submitting for your consideration.

If you, representing the Authority, and Steve Mitchell and I, representing the family agree upon this, that is an important step, but I do not believe we should consider it the final step. I believe that others should be consulted before a final decision is reached. What about the Negroes? The new hospital is for them. Would <u>they</u> like to have it called the Margaret Mitchell Marsh Memorial Hospital? I believe that you should discuss this with some of the Negro leaders. Benjamin Mays, President of Morehouse, is someone Mrs. Marsh knew and respected and there are various others whose names you will of course know.

I believe also that the newspaper editors should be consulted. They promoted public contributions to the "Margaret Mitchell Memorial" on the other basis. If a new and different plan is announced without previous consultation with them, the newspaper editors might resent it, and properly so. On the other hand, if their views are sought in advance and the circumstances are explained, they might have an entirely different attitude.

Ascertaining the wishes of the Negro leaders is important for the following reasons:

> Continuously since 1936, the Communist Party and other Red and Pink elements have been trying to put the label of "anti-Negro" on Peggy's book. The Communist newspaper in New York, The Daily Worker, still publishes frequent attacks on the book. Similar attacks, in almost identical language, have been made in Communist organs in England, Yugoslavia, Czechoslavakia, Poland and other European countries. The Reds just naturally hate everything about the book, especially its description of friendly and mutually helpful relations between white and colored people in the old South.
>
> They don't want white and colored people to get along with each other, so they have repeatedly declared that Peggy's book gives a false picture of life in the South. As a part of their scheme, they try to smear any Negroes who don't agree with them. They call such Negroes "Uncle Toms." They denounced the Negroes who had parts in the motion picture. They picketed the movie in a number of cities and the New York Daily Worker fired its motion picture critic because he refused to write a review of the movie as bad as they wanted him to write it. The effect of all of this has been, first, to cause some Negroes to believe that Peggy's book is "anti-Negro" and, second, to subject Peggy's friends among the Negroes to abuse of one kind or another. If the new hospital is named for Peggy, would that cause embarrassment to Peggy's friends among the Negroes? She would not wish them to be embarrassed, for she valued their friendship. I believe this aspect ought to be investigated, before a final decision is reached.

I wish, also, to offer some suggestions about the timing of an announcement, assuming we decided to go ahead and name the hospital for Peggy. Unless there is some urgency about the announcement, I suggest that it be withheld until a week or two after the issuance of the Atlanta Historical Society Bulletin. The Bulletin probably will be issued in about three weeks, and it will include your letter giving Peggy the credit for the idea of constructing the hospital. That will be the first public announcement that she had any part in it. I am sure it will occasion public discussion and will be commented on in the newspapers. Then, a week or two later, your announcement could be made, naming the hospital for her. This timing would, first, permit the Bulletin to get the "break" on this interesting piece of news and, second, be the proper and logical preliminary to the announcement of the naming of the hospital for her. The announcement must include a "reason why." The public is entitled to know -- Is Margaret Mitchell being honored simply because she is Margaret Mitchell? Or, is there some special fitness and justification for the action? The timing I have suggested breaks the announcement into two parts. The "reason why" comes out in the Bulletin and the naming of the hospital follows a week or two weeks later. That will be more effective from all standpoints than if you shoot off both barrels at the same time.

In conclusion, I would like to have the hospital named for Peggy, if the Negroes would like it, too. Peggy wanted them to have this hospital. She would not wish its usefulness to them to be impaired by any honor paid to her. She made a habit of subordinating herself if that would help in achieving some good objective. She would be proud to have this hospital named for her, for it meant so much to her, but not if that would make it mean less to the Negroes.

Sincerely,

John R. Marsh

cc: Mr. Stephens Mitchell

MOREHOUSE COLLEGE
Atlanta, Georgia

April 5, 1950

Office of the President

Mr. Hughes Spalding
Trust Company of Georgia Building
Atlanta, Georgia

Dear Mr. Spalding:

In keeping with our conversation last week, I thought it would be well to have a meeting of the Negro members of the committee who met with you in the initial stage of our planning for the Negro hospital. We had all members present or the opinion of everyone except one.

When we talked last week, the tragic death of Dr. Charles Drew, perhaps the most eminent Negro surgeon in America, had not occurred. The committee was unaminous in feeling that we should suggest to you that the Negro hospital be named the Charles Drew Memorial Hospital. The members of the committee feel that Charles Drew symbolized the hopes and aspirations of the Negro in America as well as anybody could and that his untimely death make due recognition of his service imperative.

As a surgeon, Charles Drew was respected by the leading surgeons of America and you know the part he played in perfecting the blood bank that saved thousands of lives on the battlefield.

The committee felt further that you, more than any other single person, made this Negro hospital a reality. In fact, you did it almost singlehandedly and we feel that some real recognition should be given to you somewhere in this program. Your modesty may make you reluctant to accept any honor, but it is certainly due you and I hope that we will have the good sense to see that due credit is given you.

Although the members of the committee feel quite kindly toward Miss Margaret Mitchell personally and appreciate the great contribution she made to the South and to literature, it is our opinion that for this purpose, Charles Drew would make a better symbol. Then too, it would be a fine thing if the South were the first to recognize the great worth of Charles Drew.

Appreciating the opportunity to do this, and with kindest regards, I am

Your truly

Benjamin E. Mays
President

BEM:dem

SPALDING, SIBLEY, TROUTMAN & KELLY
434 TRUST COMPANY OF GEORGIA BUILDING

April 6,1950

Mr. John R. Marsh
1268 Piedmont Avenue
Atlanta 5, Georgia

Mr. Stephens Mitchell
Peters Building
Atlanta 3, Georgia

Dear John & Steve:

I wrote you recently about the name for the new Negro Hospital. John told me when I discussed the matter with him on the telephone that he wanted the opinion of Benjamin E. Mays, President of Morehouse College. I talked to Mays and in my recent letter gave a resume of what he and others had to say.

This morning I am in receipt of a letter from Dr. Mays, copy of which I enclose to each of you. I thought you should have the benefit of his thinking prior to our meeting on Saturday.

Personal wishes to each of you.

Sincerely yours,

Hughes Spalding

HS:RM
Enclosure

1268 Piedmont Avenue, N.E.
Atlanta 5, Georgia

April 10, 1950

Mr. Hughes Spalding
Fulton-DeKalb Hospital Authority
Atlanta 3, Georgia

Dear Mr. Spalding:

I have received a copy of the letter to you from Dr. Mays in which he objects to the name of Margaret Mitchell being used as the name of the new pay hospital for Negroes.

I had written you that the hospital could be named for her, provided that was the desire both of the Hospital Authority and of the Negroes of Atlanta. The hospital is being built for the Negroes, so I felt that their ideas should be obtained.

A number of Atlanta's Negroes have said they are in favor of the proposal. Dr. Mays and all but one of his committee are not in favor of it. In view of this disagreement, I do not think Mrs. Marsh's name should be used.

Getting the hospital built is what she wanted. That it might be named for her, would not have entered her mind. In fact, I cannot imagine her consenting to it unless there was an almost unanimous public demand for it. Personal honors were not what she wanted, and I know she would not have permitted herself to be honored in connection with this hospital if that would cause public disagreements and controversy, and perhaps impair the usefulness of the hospital.

In light of the substantial disagreement already expressed, my tentative permission for the use of her name is withdrawn. I have discussed this with Stephens Mitchell and he joins me in this action.

Sincerely,
John R. Marsh

cc: Mr. Stephens Mitchell

(File notes) April 28, 1950

Dr. Benjamin Mays, of Morehouse College, came to see me this afternoon and discussed various matters as follows:

G. Bennett Trust

1. Our interpretation of the provisions of the Grady Bennett Trust Fund - I told him it was still available to Grady if he entered medical school by September 1950. It is highly improbable that he will do so, he has given up the idea of being a doctor, he has not been following the pre-medical course and Dr. Mays said he probably could not obtain admission to a medical school because he does not have a very good scholastic record. He is doing reasonably well but the medical schools now refuse to take anybody without an excellent scholastic record.

C. Mitchell Fund Morehouse

2. The Carrie Mitchell Holbrook Fund, to which Peggy donated $2,000, has not yet been put into use as a scholarship. Dr. Mays asked if I thought it would be proper for him to use the accumulated interest to provide scholarship help for some three or four Morehouse graduates now at Meharry. I told him I did not think this would be prohibited by the terms of the scholarship but that it would not be in keeping with the spirit of it. It specifies that the money is to be used for "a student" who wishes to study medicine and practice in a Southern state. It would therefore seem proper that an effort should be made to devote the fund to some student fitting the specifications instead of to dissipate it in contributions to students in general.

3. I had thanked Dr. Mays for his column about Peggy in the Pittsburg Courier last August when I found that he had brought a copy of it with him to show me. It paid a high tribute to her as a person as well as an author.

Negro hosp. file with H. Spalding

4. The naming of the new pay hospital for Negroes came up almost incidentally. He had not been notified of our withdrawal of Peggy's name and I told him the situation. We had a pleasant discussion of the matter in which he praised her helpfulness to the Negroes but thought it would be better to name the hospital for a Negro. I told him that the simple matter of lack of agreement among the Negroes was my reason for withdrawing her name, that I thought it should not be used unless there was an almost unanimous demand for it, and that I had no hard feelings about the position he had taken.

comments

5. The trend of the above discussion convinced me that he had no awareness of the Red angles, and I decided to tell him that nothing would make the Communists happier than a wrangle among the Negroes about Peggy. He expressed surprise, and I think he was sincere when I told him of the Communist line when I said they had worked industriously to label the book "anti-Negro," he responded "But it is not." If I am any judge, the whole aspect of Communist dislike of the book was news to him.

September 1, 1950

Mr. John Marsh
1268 Piedmont Avenue, N.E.
Atlanta, GEorgia

Dear Mr. Marsh:

You are a friend to Morehouse. And it is for this reason that I am sending you a copy of "Then and Now" which is a Summary of my Ten Years at Morehouse College.

You would do me a great favor if you would take a few moments of your time and read this brief document through. Please do it. And if you should feel inclined to give me your reaction to this report, I would love it.

With kindest regards and best wishes always, I am

Yours truly,

Benjamin E. Mays
President

BEM:aw

N.B. I hope you will give me your reactions to this report.
B.E.M.

**THE CITIZENS & SOUTHERN NATIONAL BANK
ATLANTA, GA.**

Dr. Benjamin Mays, President
Morehouse College
Atlanta, Georgia

Dear Dr. Mays:

For your information, there is enclosed a copy of a trust agreement between this bank and Mrs. Margaret Mitchell Marsh entered into August 21, 1946. Grady Bennett, referred to therein, did not enter Meharry Medical College, or any other medical college, and expressed in writing his intention not to accept the funds of the trust for the purpose outlined therein. Accordingly, the funds revert to you in your official capacity as President of Morehouse College, in trust for purposes as stated in paragraph 3 of the agreement. We shall appreciate hearing from you at your convenience with respect to your receiving delivery of the funds.

Very truly yours,

A. M. Adamson
Vice President

AMA:dtg

Enc.

January 25, 1951

Mr. John Marsh
1268 Piedmont Avenue, N.E.
Atlanta, Georgia

Dear Mr. Marsh:

I have placed in the Citizens Trust Company the sum of $3,155.78 in an account with Dr. Benjamin E. Mays as Trustee of the Margaret Mitchell Scholarship Fund. I thought I should report to you just how the money is banked and I will also keep you informed as to its distribution.

I hope you are well and sometime in the not too distant future, I will want to talk with you again.

With kindest regards and best wishes, I am

Yours truly,

Benjamin E. Mays
President

BEM:H

January 26, 1951

Dr. Benjamin E. Mays, President
Morehouse College
Atlanta, Georgia

Dear Dr. Mays:

I am glad to learn from your letter of January 25 that the transfer of the Margaret Mitchell Marsh Scholarship Fund has been effected and that the money is now on deposit in the Citizens Trust Company. I shall welcome further information from you as to the distribution of the fund. Mrs. Marsh was sincerely hopeful that this money would do good, and she would have wished to know what was done with it.

I am feeling better these days and it would be a pleasure to talk with you again. With best regards

Sincerely yours,

John R. Marsh

January 29, 1951

Mr. John R. Marsh
1268 Piedmont Avenue, N.E.
Atlanta 5, Georgia

Dear Mr. Marsh:

I appreciate your letter of January 26th. We could move a little faster in distributing the Margaret Mitchell Marsh Scholarship Fund, but we want to be certain that the right person is helped with the hope that the greatest amount of good is done.

Rest assured that I feel an obligation to keep you informed. With kindest regards and best wishes, I am

Yours truly,

Benjamin E. Mays
President

BEM:kl

3113 11th St. N.W.
Washington, D.C.

May 26, 1951

Dear Mr. Marsh,

This is to express my gratitude and appreciation for a sum of money I received which was made possible through your wife's efforts. The money, fifty dollars, is from a contribution given by your wife to Morehouse College in order to (help) some Morehouse student in medical school each year. Reiterating my gratefulness while closing, I remain,

Yours truly,

Benj. H. Barbour

June 25, 1951

Mr. Benjamin H. Barbour
3113 Eleventh St., N.W.
Washington, D.C.

Dear Mr. Barbour:

It was gratifying to me to have your letter thanking me for the money you received from the fund my wife established to help students at Morehouse College. I know Mrs. Marsh, too, would have been pleased by your letter, so I thank you on her behalf as well.

My best wishes to you for the future.

Sincerely yours,

John R. Marsh

September 7, 1951

Mr. John R. Marsh
26 Walker Terrace, NE
Atlanta 5,
Georgia

Dear Mr. Marsh:

I appreciate your sending me a copy of the letter which you received from Mr. William E. Finlayson. I am very glad he wrote you. I feel that everybody should be grateful for anything that anyone does for him or her that they do not have to do. I am very happy to note that Mr. Finlayson wrote you.

I have just returned from Europe where I attended the Central Committee meeting of the World Council of Churches. I enjoyed my visit to see you some months ago and I may be coming out to see you again in the not too distant future.

With kindest regards and best wishes, I am

Yours truly,

Benjamin E. Mays
President

BEM:dem

Meharry Medical College
Nashville, Tenn.
October 14, 1951

Mr. John R. Marsh
1268 Piedmont Ave NE
Atlanta, Georgia

Dear Mr. Marsh:

Introducing myself, I am Clarence G. Littlejohn, junior medical student of Meharry Medical College and 1949 graduate of Morehouse College in Atlanta. I was one of the recipients of the scholarship aid made possible thru Morehouse College by the generosity and understanding of your wife, Mrs. Margaret Mitchell Marsh. Dr. Mays has acquainted me with the exemplary spirit she displayed by establishing such a fund to be used to aid young students of medicine who plan to practice in the South.

I am indeed grateful for the admirable deed your wife did and wish to show my appreciation - for such aid came to me when a financial crisis threatened the financial structure of my medical education. My anemic resources had begun sagging and I was spending much of my time (which should have been allotted to studies) racking my brain trying to think of ways and means to pull myself out of my financial rut. Strangely enough, there are few scholarships offered to medical students, I found out upon applying to many. And working after school (like I did at Morehouse) is out of the question if you want to learn at least 3/4 of the material tossed at you in texts and classrooms. So you see, the scholarship aid was a life saver. I shall do my utmost to prove myself worthy of having received it.

Thanks. With kindest regards, I am

Very truly yours,

Clarence G. Littlejohn

October 24, 1951

Mr. Clarence G. Littlejohn
Meharry Medical College
Nashville, Tennessee

Dear Mr. Littlejohn:

Thank you for your letter of October 14, in which you say that you are one of those helped by the fund Mrs. Marsh established. She would have been sincerely pleased by your letter, and for her sake I am too. She wanted to aid Morehouse students seeking a medical education and, in your case, it seems that the aid came at a critical time.

It was kind of you to write as you did, and I appreciate it. My very best wishes for the successful completion of your studies.

Sincerely yours,

John R. Marsh

cc: Dr. Benjamin Mays

(Christmas card from the Mays, Christmas, 1951)

Christmas 1951

The Season's Greetings

We dedicate ourselves anew to these ideals:

Our dream is of peace and good will
and for these we will strive.

Our prayer is for brotherhood
and for brotherhood we will work.

Our desire is social justice for all peoples in every land.

Our goal is democracy
and we will implement democracy by living it.

President and Mrs. Benjamin E. Mays

Morehouse College, Atlanta, Georgia

MOREHOUSE COLLEGE
Atlanta, Georgia

February 13, 1952

Mr. John R. Marsh
26 Walker Terrace, NE
Atlanta, Georgia

Dear Mr. Marsh:

It was kind of you to see me when I was out to your residence the other day. At that time I promised to send you a lay-out of the lounge which we hope to provide on the first floor of the chemistry building for the men of Morehouse. The lay-out is enclosed. As I stated in my conversation with you we have no social-educational-center where our men and faculty can gather.

The room will be used as a conference room and for social purposes. We have no where now except the President's Residence for the entertaining of small groups that come to the campus. We have no conference room for the exclusive use of Morehouse faculty. It will really be a combination of lounge and conference room.

I agree with you that to put in as much as six or seven thousand dollars worth of equipment is very high. It will certainly be more elaborate than anything Morehouse has at the present. In suggesting that figure, as I discussed it with a committee here at the college, I had two things in mind.

1. We would want the room to be equipped with the best material that would last a long time. We want it to be beautiful as well as useful.

2. If you could see your way clear to equip the room in which case it would be a room in memory of Mrs. Marsh, I thought it should be equipped with the very best material. As you said in your conversation with me, to equip a room

as expensive as that might not be in keeping with the simplicity with which Mrs. Marsh lived. I can quite understand your feelings in that matter. I am also conscious of the fact that the room could be equipped more cheaply, but I doubt if it could be equipped with the kind of material we need with high prices for less than four or five thousand dollars.

If you can see your way clear to do this for Morehouse in memory of Miss Mitchell, we would be forever grateful to you. She had an interest in and concern for all peoples. She certainly had manifested that interest in Negroes by what she had already done at Morehouse. I believe it would be a fitting thing for her to be memorialized in some such fashion in a negro institution. I shall look forward to hearing from you at your first opportunity.

With kindest regards, I am

Yours truly,

Benjamin E. Mays
President

BEM:dem

N.B. *If you are interested, please feel free to make suggestions. The size of the lounge is on lay-out 2.*

February 20, 1952

Dr. Benjamin E. Mays, President
Morehouse College
Atlanta, Georgia

Dear Dr. Mays:

I have thought over your proposal that I pay for the furnishing of the new students' lounge and conference room at Morehouse as a memorial to Mrs. Marsh. I read your letter of February 13 and examined the layouts with interest. I am sorry to tell you that I have decided this is not the kind of memorial I would like to establish. The idea of the lounge is good, but I believe it is not as appropriate as something else might be as a memorial to my wife. She was a useful person, and her contributions and work went into simple and "useful" channels. By this I do not mean to imply that the lounge would not be useful. I know the value and need of a room such as you have planned, but after much study I do not warm up to it as the kind of memorial I would choose, simply because there is no way in which it symbolizes or suggests the kind of person she was and the life she lived. At a later date, I might consider making a contribution for some other purpose.

I am returning herewith the two layouts, as you may have some use for them.

Sincerely yours,

John R. Marsh

2 Enclosures.

MOREHOUSE COLLEGE
Atlanta, Georgia

February 26, 1952

Mr. John R. Marsh
26 Walker Terrace, NE
Atlanta 5,
Georgia

Dear Mr. Marsh:

I have been away one week participating in a Religion in Life Week at Bucknell University in Pennsylvania and this accounts for my delay in answering your letter of February 20.

I can quite understand how you feel relative to the request which I made of you. After talking with you in your home, I felt that you probably did not want to memorialize Mrs. Marsh in that way. I am not at all disappointed. I certainly would not want anything to be done that was not in keeping with the fine useful life which Mrs. Marsh lived.

If, at a later time, you can see your way clear to make a contribution for some other purpose we shall be grateful.

With kindest regards and best wishes, I am

Yours truly,

Benjamin E. Mays
President

BEM:dem

MOREHOUSE COLLEGE
Atlanta, Georgia

May 14, 1957

Mr. Stephens Mitchell
Atlanta Federal Savings Building
Broad and Marietta Streets
Atlanta, Georgia

Dear Mr. Mitchell:

I still remember the very pleasant conversation which I had in your office a few months ago. I hope I may be privileged to come back and talk to you further at some time in the not too distant future.

At that time you thought it would be possible for you to make a contribution to Morehouse College about April 15th. Since we are trailing behind in our finances for our $850,000 physical education and health building, any amount you contribute will be greatly apprciated.

With kindest regards and best wishes, I am

Yours truly,

Benjamin E. Mays
President

BEM:H

N.B. *I would love to memorialize Miss Mitchell in some way.*

IN BUSINESS NINETY YEARS BUILDING MEN

June 14, 1957

Dr. Benjamin E. Mays, President
Morehouse College
223 Chestnut Street, S.W.
Atlanta, Georgia

Dear Dr. Mays:

I received your letter of May 14, and was happy to talk with you when you called at my office. I am sorry that at the present time I am not in position to make a donation to Morehouse. I shall keep the matter in mind, however, and hope that I shall be able to do something along this line at some future date.

Sincerely,

Stephens Mitchell

MOREHOUSE COLLEGE
Atlanta, Georgia

June 20, 1957

Mr. Stephens Mitchell
412 Peachtree Arcade
Atlanta 3, Georgia

Dear Mr. Mitchell:

I thank you for your kind letter of June 14.

I appreciate the fact that you still have Morehouse in mind and that at some future date you hope to be able to do something for the College. One fact is clear - a college is always in need and when you see your way clear to make a contribution it will be greatly needed and highly appreciated.

Sincerely yours,

Benjamin E. Mays
President

BEM:J

IN BUSINESS NINETY YEARS BUILDING MEN

III
THE MARGARET MITCHELL SCHOLARS

It is important to keep in mind that some former students and alumni of Morehouse College came from families that could afford to support their education in medicine or dentistry. The majority, though, needed help. We want to profile the careers of some of the latter group, doctors who received aid as a direct result of the Mitchell-Mays connection. It is difficult to profile all of them; for some have either passed away, have addresses that are unknown, or were otherwise not in the position to participate in our survey. However, there is one Margaret Mitchell Scholar whom we had no difficulty reaching, for he has maintained an active, visible role in the Atlanta community, including Vice chairman and membership on the board of the Margaret Mitchell House, Inc. We single him out as an example of the numerous scholars and humanitarians who benefited directly from the Mays-Mitchell legacy.

He is well known to most of the others and resides in Atlanta, where he, like most of them, has had a stellar record of achievement. His name is Otis W. Smith, better known to generations of Morehouse men as "Will Shoot." The nickname does two things. It refers to his demonstrated ability with the basketball, and it also suggests what invariably happened to any basketball that found itself in his capable hands.

Born in Atlanta, Otis Smith was twelve years old in 1939, the year of the premiere of "Gone With The Wind." That year, Smith now says, "I prayed to God that he would make me a doctor."

Otis's father was Ralph Smith, a large, muscular man who stood six feet tall and weighed over two hundred pounds. A hard-working man, Ralph took pride in his family, duty, and love of God. The family was determined to overcome the obstacles facing most black Atlantans of that era: racism, segregation, poverty, and lack of education. The family suffered racism in the medical profession that left an indelible impression on young Otis. His father took sick. After being treated by a white doctor in Atlanta, the elder Smith underwent major surgery and was sent home to die. The insensitive white doctor had failed to properly close the wound. The responsibility for nursing his father back to health fell upon young Otis, the youngest child and only boy. There in the back room of the family home, Otis Smith's tears, courage, and experiences transformed boy into man, a man who had found his calling in the world. He treated his father as best he could for the remaining eight months of Ralph Smith's life.

Eight years later, Otis entered Morehouse College assured that the Lord had called him to heal the body in the same way that he called others to heal the soul. He just had to be a doctor. He told Dr. Mays about his mental rendezvous with the will of God. While at Morehouse, Smith achieved the distinction of being the only athlete in the college's history to letter in four sports: baseball, football, track, and basketball.

After entering Meharry Medical School, Otis found himself without funds for the second year's expenses. He wrote to his mentor, Dr. Mays. Armed with Margaret Mitchell's money, "Buck Bennie" rode to the rescue; and Smith was saved. Another element of Smith's salvation, however, was a phenomenon known as "The Farm." Starting in the 1920s, in a program among whose major sponsors was Morehouse College, generations of southern boys and young men rode north every summer on such railroad lines as the Southern and the Seaboard to work on tobacco farms in such Connecticut towns as Bloomfield, Simsbury, Granby, and

Buckland. Smith may have established the all-time record for this income- producing activity with twelve consecutive summers spent "picking tobacco," serving as foreman of a group of tobacco workers, or shooting basketball.

Dr. Smith, after completing his medical education, practiced pediatrics for a while in Fort Valley, Georgia, and then returned to Atlanta, to finish his medical career. To assist others, Dr. Smith donated $50,000 to Morehouse College at his class reunion in 1987. Dr. Smith and four others played a pivotal role in integrating Atlanta's hospital establishment in the late 1960s.

Three Morehouse alumni, Drs. James E. Ellison, Albert Davis, and Otis Smith, chairperson of the committee, and two others, Mrs. Xernona Clayton, now of Turner Enterprises, and Dr. Roy C. Bell, now of Washington, D.C., completed the group. Knowing that white hospitals were not in compliance with regulations of the Department of Health, Education, and Welfare (HEW), the group, identified as The Committee on Implementation because their goal was to implement federal law, challenged HEW and even Congress. Eventually, their efforts in Atlanta and Washington, D.C. opened up Atlanta's white hospitals to Blacks. The team of five is credited with breaking the back of racial segregation in medical facilities for medical practioners and patients not just in Atlanta, but throughout the country.

Like Dr. Otis Smith, several other Morehouse alumni were able to realize their dreams and help society partly because of assistance from Margaret Mitchell. Additional profiles of some of the Mays-Mitchell scholarship recipients offer just a glimpse of the high accomplishments of a group of determined black men. Most of them never knew about the Margaret Mitchell involvement until they learned about it within the last year or so from Ira Joe Johnson. Mitchell had virtually sworn Mays to secrecy. Johnson documents the link between Mitchell and Morehouse with archival letters, interviews, and other independent records. Each of these doctors or dentists met the criteria of need and character set by Mitchell and Mays. Among them, we find the following specialties: urology, nephrology, pediatrics, surgery, psychiatry, and pathology. All had Morehouse experience, all except two obtained the bachelor's degree at Morehouse, and all finished medical or dental school at Meharry or Howard. These medical practitioners have indeed healed thousands of the sick and contributed immensely to society. Mays, Mitchell, and the nation can be proud of them.

Authors' note: The primary sources of information about the careers of the Margaret Mitchell Scholars are the doctors themselves, by way of questionnaires, short autobiographies, published material, interviews, or other sources thought to be fully reliable. Varying amounts of information was received, so some entries are short. If there are errors, they are of the head and not the heart.

Sam Oillie Atkins, M.D.
UROLOGIST
Atlanta, Georgia

Dr. Atkins attended Morehouse from 1945-47 and earned the bachelor's in 1953 at the University of Buffalo. He earned his medical degree at Howard University in1957. Then he went on to do internships and residencies in other urban centers: Cleveland Metropolitan General Hospital, Cleveland, Ohio; Mercy Douglas Hospital, Philadelphia, PA; and Akron General Hospital, Akron, Ohio. Dr. Atkins has further distinguished himself as Chief Urologist, U.S. Army Hospital, 196th Station Hospital, Supreme Headquarters for Allied Powers of Europe, Belgium; as Associate Chief of Urology, Martin Army Hospital, Columbus, Georgia; as Officer-in-Charge, Physical Exam Section,Fort MacPherson Army Post, East Point, Georgia; and as Associate Professor of Surgery, Urology, Morehouse School of Medicine.

He was Chief Resident Surgeon at the Bronx Municipal Hospital Center in New York and at the Boston City Hospital, Boston University Medical Center. Actually, his list of hospital appointments calls for more space than we have. The publisher of eighteen articles, Dr. Atkins has been in private practice with Dr. Delutha King, Southwest Urology Associates, since 1971.

Benjamin Atkinson, D.D.S.
DENTIST
Miami, Florida

Dr. Atkinson finished Morehouse in 1948. Having learned in recent years about the assistance of Margaret Mitchell, he states, "I was very happy and curious to know the details." He adds that he has responded to the opportunity to practice medicine by "providing medical care to the indigent and inner city citizens." According to an edition of the Morehouse College Alumni Directory, Dr. Atkinson earned the D.D.S in 1953 and maintained a family practice in dentistry in Miami, Florida until his death over a year ago.

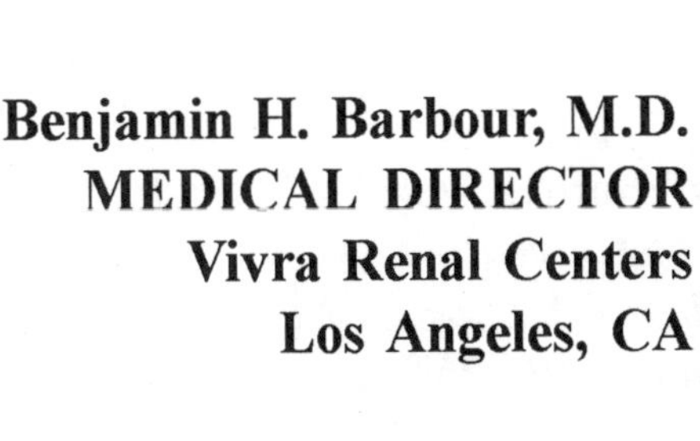

Benjamin H. Barbour, M.D.
MEDICAL DIRECTOR
Vivra Renal Centers
Los Angeles, CA

Dr. Barbour finished Morehouse in 1948 and then earned the M.D. from Meharry in 1952. He did an internship and residency at Los Angeles County General Hospital, serving as Chief Medical Resident at the University of California Service, Los Angeles County General Hospital, Los Angeles, California. For two years he was a medical officer in the United States Air Force, with the rank of Captain. He held many posts at the University of Southern California, including assistant and associate professor of medicine. Presently, he is medical director of Vivra Renal Centers in Los Angeles.

Dr. Barbour states:

> *Today I spoke with Ira J. Johnson regarding his upcoming book about the life of Dr. Benjamin Mays.... Dr. Mays was an awesome figure in my mind. I had the greatest respect for him while I attended Morehouse, and my memory of him always placed him as a great man. Dr. Mays was a source of inspiration to me. He was like an alter-ego for me, inspiring a sense of self-confidence towards mankind's well being. Even today I often recall his homilies as a great source of wisdom.*

Dr. Barbour was apparently one of the few who knew of the Margaret Mitchell element in the assistance that he received. He wrote the following letter to John Marsh two years after Mitchell's death.

> *Dear Mr. Marsh,*
>
> *This is to express my gratitude and appreciation for a sum of money I received which was made possible through your wife's efforts. The money, fifty dollars, is from a contribution given by your wife to Morehouse College in order to [help] some Morehouse student in medical school each year.*
>
> *Reiterating my gratefulness while closing, I remain,*
>
> *Yours truly,*
>
> *Benj. H. Barbour*

The letter is dated May 26, 1951, the year before Dr. Barbour finished Meharry. It is hard to find clearer documentation than this letter provides of the Mitchell program of giving to Morehouse.

Everett L. Dargan, M.D.
THORACIC/ VASCULAR SURGEON
Columbia, South Carolina

Dr. Dargan attended Morehouse for two years (1945-1947). He received the bachelor's degree from the University of Buffalo and the M.D. from Howard. He did residencies in surgery at several New York hospitals and served as Chief Resident Surgeon at Bronx Municipal Hospital Center. Also, he was Chief Resident Surgeon at Boston City Hospital, Boston University Medical Center. Dr. Dargan is certified to practice medicine in New York, South Carolina, and Massachusetts. He has published eighteen articles during his medical career.

Dr. Dargan recalled receiving financial assistance as well as spiritual inspiration from the kindness and wisdom of Dr. Mays. Noting that Dr. Mays never seemed to forget a Morehouse student that he encountered, Dargan recalled that Dr. Mays wrote a letter of congratulations to him after he became the first Black Chief Resident Surgeon at the Bronx Municipal Hospital Center.

Dr. Dargan was born in Columbia, South Carolina, and spent his entire childhood there. It was, he says, "a rigidly segregated society with a stifling and oppressive atmosphere; but he had parents who had instilled in him the desire to succeed and excel." Inspired also by his teachers, he became convinced that "Knowledge is Power" and that knowledge would liberate him in spite of his beginnings. He writes interestingly of his childhood, calling it typical: "I played with pet chickens and frogs, rode bicycles, and played baseball, basketball, and football." He toyed with the idea of becoming a plumber or a professional baseball player until he realized that in 1945 there were no licensed black plumbers in South Carolina nor black major league baseball players. Encouraged by his teachers, he, along with others, took a national scholarship examination for early entrance into college. Successful with the examination, he entered Morehouse at age fifteen. He calls the Morehouse experience "a defining moment in my development." Morehouse exposed him to a new world and the joys and power of knowledge.

Transferring to the University of Buffalo after two years, he obtained the Baccalaureate Degree there. He spent the next four years at Howard University School of Medicine where he was exposed to the teachings and philosophies of Drs. John B. Johnson and Charles R. Drew. He did his internship and residency at the institutions mentioned above, spending two years in the U.S. Air Force in the interim. He was stationed in England with the 391th USAF Airbase Group and served as Base Surgeon and Hospital Commander, "broadening and enlightening" experiences. He completed his training in Thoracic and Cardiovascular Surgery at the Boston University Medical Center and returned to the Albert Einstein Medical Center where he became Assistant Professor of Surgery first, then Associate Professor of Surgery, and then Acting Director of Surgery at its Lincoln Hospital affiliate.

Selected by the Health and Hospitals Corporation of New York City, he became Director of Surgery at its Sydenham Hospital with a mandate to elevate the practice of surgery there. After four years, Dr. Dargan was offered the Chairmanship of the Department of Surgery at the King-Drew Medical Center in Los Angeles. Feeling very concerned about the state of surgery in African American communities on the East coast, he declined the California position, returned to his native South Carolina, a move that would probably have pleased Margaret Mitchell, and established a surgical practice, Midlands Surgical Associates, P.A. With a surgical staff of four African Americans and a limitation to Thoracic, Vascular, and General surgery, it is "one of the largest and most successful associations of African American surgeons in the South."

In his home state, he has served in numerous other capacities. Among them are the past presidency of the Palmetto Medical, Dental, and Pharmaceutical Association; Board of Trustees of the Richland Memorial Hospital Center; and a founding member of the Physician's Health Plan of South Carolina, a managed care company. Also, he is a member of the Executive Board and is Secretary/Treasurer of the physician-directed Health Plan Company of South Carolina.

In the community, Dr. Dargan has been a director of the American Red Cross Association and the American Cancer Society. He has been a director of the Victory Savings Bank in Columbia, S.C. A trustee of his church, he is a life member of the NAACP. It is his "fervent desire" that more African Americans will enter the medical profession and serve in a "competent, compassionate, and caring" environment, traits which show that he believed as Margaret Mitchell did. Dr. Dargan is married to the former Carol Poyner. They have two daughters.

M. Delmar Edwards, M.D.
SURGEON
Columbus, Georgia

No Photo Available

Dr. Edwards attended Morehouse and went on to earn the B.S. degree at Central State University in Wilberforce, Ohio, in 1948. He received a Master's from Atlanta University in 1952. After earning the M.D., he interned at Reynolds Memorial Hospital in Winston Salem, North Carolina, followed by a surgery internship at the Medical Center in Columbus, Georgia. That residency was completed at the Veterans Administration Hospital in Tuskegee, Alabama. Since 1966 he has been on the staff at the Medical Center in Columbus, Georgia. For a period he was Chairman of the Department of Surgery there.

In the book, I Swear By Apollo, he was discussed by a colleague, Dr. S.A. Roddenbery. Dr. Roddenbery writes of himself: "Having been born and reared in Georgia, I learned at an early age to hate Yankees and Negroes" (Roddenbery 10). This point of view of a white southerner is suggested by Dr. Roddenbery birth in Macon, Georgia. In four years at the University of Georgia and another four years at Harvard Medical School, he "never saw or had contact with a black student." These comments by a white doctor from the South should help us to see what black people were up against in the South in the 1940s, the main period of schooling of the scholarship recipients. Dr. Roddenbery had a chance for growth in 1964 when a Morehouse man, Dr. Delmar Edwards, appeared in his office. Dr. Roddenbery and his partner, Dr. Abe Conger, were working to build their practices in surgery and had no incentive to delve in controversial matters. Still, they had to make a decision when Dr. Edwards asked them to be his preceptors for a further two year period of surgical residency. Since they knew of Dr. Edwards's work because of their roles as consultants to Tuskegee Veterans Hospital, where they knew that Dr. Edwards had successfully completed three years of surgical residency, they decided to accept the preceptor roles.

The reviewer informs us, based apparently on Dr. Roddenbery's book, that Dr. Edwards was born in Arkansas. He took a B.S. degree from Wilberforce University in 1948, took an extra year at Morehouse, and spent two years in the U.S. Navy as a medical corpsman. Setting out to become a surgeon, he taught at a number of colleges and earned a master's from Atlanta University. All the time his objective was the University of Arkansas Medical School; it took him five years. The account continues:

> *He had to deal with every shade of discrimination. Fortunately, growing up in a segregated society had taught him how to accept without servility but with dignified composure the reality of barbs, scorn and racial prejudice, not allowing them to distract him from his long-range goals* (10).

In 1957 Dr. Edwards became the fifth black student to graduate from the University of Arkansas Medical School. Still, the long road to surgical training lay ahead: a one-year rotating internship in Winston-Salem and three years of general practice in Fort Smith, Arkansas, to repay a man who had also helped with his medical education. Eventually, he went to the Veteran's Administration Hospital in Tuskegee (10). Dr. Roddenbery wrote in the epilogue to his book:

> *From the beginning, it was obvious to Abe and me that in his daily living, Delmar would do everything within his power to create a situation in which young, well-trained black physicians who followed him would not suffer any of the indignities or deprivations he had experienced*(11).

The reviewer of Dr. Roddenbery's book writes, "They never had cause to regret their decision."

With inspiration that he attributes to Dr. Mays, Dr. Edwards has sought to give back to his community throughout his career. He is a member of numerous civic and professional organizations.

Both he and his son, Dr. Delmar Edwards, Jr. are presently on the faculty at the Morehouse School of Medicine in Atlanta, Georgia.

Dr. Edwards and his wife Betty have three children.

Dr. William E. Finlayson
OBSTETRICS/ GYNECOLOGY
Milwaukee, Wisconsin

No Photo Available

Dr. Finlayson finished Morehouse in 1948 and Howard in 1953, according to the Morehouse College Alumni Directory and the questionnaire he returned. He practices in Milwaukee, Wisconsin. In his questionnaire he states, "The records show that I was mentioned in a letter by Dr. Mays and Mitchell's husband." The records he refers to are ones he learned of from author Johnson. About his initial reaction, he says, "I couldn't believe it. Mr. Johnson had to convince me by faxing me proof." About his own attitude toward giving, he states, "I have felt and was taught by Dr. Mays that to whom much is given, much is expected and required."

Bernard F. Gipson, Sr., M.D.
GENERAL SURGERY
Denver, Colorado

Dr. Gipson, born in Bivins, Texas, finished Morehouse in 1944. He received the M.D. from Howard in 1947 and then interned at Harlem Hospital in New York and Freedmen's Hospital at the Howard University Medical Center, Washington D.C. His surgical residency was done at Howard under the direction of the famed Dr. Charles R. Drew. A general surgeon, Dr. Gipson has taught surgery at several hospitals and medical centers, including the University of Colorado in Denver. He is certified to practice medicine in Colorado, District of Columbia, Maryland, and Texas.

According to information supplied to us, he has been one of the prime moving forces in helping to integrate hospital staffs and in bringing black physicians and surgeons into the mainstream of medical practice in the Denver, Colorado, area. He was the first Black man in his county to graduate from medical school. His election to the medical school honorary scholastic society, Kappa Pi, attests to his superior academic ability. Dr. Gipson became a diplomate of the American Board of Surgery.

Dr. Gipson went to Denver as a medical officer in the U.S. Air Force and was assigned to Lowry Air Force Base. He served there as Chief of Surgery. Upon completion of his tour in the Air Force, he entered private practice in surgery in Denver. He is a fellow of the American College of Surgeons, member of the National Medical Association and the American Medical Association. He retired as a Clinical Associate Professor of Surgery at the University of Colorado Health Sciences Center.

Dr. Gipson has been a community worker. He has been recognized for outstanding community service in the area of health care by several organizations. He is a member of the Owl Club of Denver and Kappa Alpha Psi fraternity. He and his wife, Ernestine, have two children, Bernard F. Gipson, Jr., M.D. and Bruce Gipson. So, here is one of several cases in which the Mitchell-Mays connection spawned two generations of medical practioners. The senior Gipsons have two grandchildren.

Consider, though, how easy it could have been for Dr. Gipson, Sr. to miss his chance for a medical career in the first place. He tells the story:

> *Dr. Benjamin E. Mays is responsible for my becoming a physician. I was at Morehouse from 1942 to 1944, during World War II. I had completed all of my premedical requirements to enter medical school, but my local board in Texas would not defer me to enter medical school.*
>
> *My application was at both Howard and Meharry, but I had not been accepted. The law was that if one had completed all of the requirements for medical school one should be deferred to study medicine and enter the military as a medical officer.*
>
> *Mrs. Sadie Mays, Dr. Mays's wife, had me over for breakfast before I left Morehouse to return to Texas to enter the army. She was terribly upset that I was not being allowed*

to continue my medical education as the law stated. Dr. Mays was in New York City when I left Morehouse to enter the army, and Mrs. Mays called him and explained my situation to him. Dr. Mays called Colonel Campbell Johnson, who was an African American officer in the Pentagon in Washington, and explained the situation. Colonel Johnson advised him to see if he could get me admitted at Howard and to call him back. Dr. Mays called Dr. John Lawlah, who was a Morehouse graduate and dean of Howard's medical school. I was accepted over the telephone at midnight.

The next morning Dr. Mays called Colonel Campbell Johnson back and notified him of my acceptance for the March class of 1944 at Howard University. Colonel Johnson then sent a telegram to Austin, Texas, which is the capital, and told the officials that when I arrived home to send me back to Morehouse so that I could enter Howard. I graduated from Howard Medical School in 1947 in the top ten of my class of eighty-five.

Dr. Mays married me and my wife (Ernestine Wallace) of Atlanta, Spelman class of 1943, in Sale Hall Chapel, Dec. 19, 1947. He visited us when I was training in New York and Washington, D.C., always encouraging us. Dr. Mays, as you can see, had a great influence on my life.

An excellent article by Sandra Dillard-Rosen about Dr. Gipson has been published in Business Emporium. The article, "Pioneer Physician," refers to him as a "surgeon, a family doctor, father figure, 'psychiatrist,' and friend to thousands of Denver-area Blacks."

Dr. Gipson credits Dr. Mays for helping him to get into medical school, but was, of course, unaware of the source of funds which helped to keep him there.

Clarence Gosha
DENTIST
Savannah, Georgia

No Photo Available

Dr. Gosha finished Morehouse College in 1949 and the Meharry School of Medicine in 1953. On his questionnaire, Dr. Gosha tells us that he has mixed emotions about the Mitchell assistance: "On the one hand it is good to hear that Dr. Mays and Ms. Mitchell were helpful and sad that I didn't know earlier." In reference to the question concerning his own generosity, he says, "I always felt a need to help others."

Arthur R. Henderson, M.D.
PSYCHIATRIST
Washington, D.C.

Dr. Henderson finished Morehouse in 1944 with the B.S. degree and received another B.S. from Howard in 1947. He received the M.D. from Meharry and did internships and residencies at McKeesport Hospital in McKeesport, PA., Western Psychiatric Institute and Clinic, University of Pittsburg, and did post-graduate medical study at the University of Buffalo, Buffalo, N.Y. Dr. Henderson has held many positions, including professor in the Department of Psychiatry at the University of Pittsburg and D.C. General Hospital. He currently serves as Assistant Clinical Professor in the Department of Psychiatry at Howard University.

According to his biography, Dr. Henderson has practiced medicine and psychiatry in Washington, D.C. for thirty- five years. He specializes in psychotherapy, chemotherapy, hypnosis, biofeedback, and other adult treatment modalities. He is a recognized expert in the treatment of acute psychiatric illness in hospital in-patients as well as in private practice. Because of his early training as a pharmacist prior to medical school, Dr. Henderson has pioneered and is regarded as an expert in the field of psychochemotherapy. One of the first Washington area psychiatrists to use hypnosis and biofeedback in the treatment of anxiety disorders, Dr. Henderson, together with two colleagues, founded the Psychiatric Center. Chartered in 1972, it is a day hospital that specializes in psychiatric assessments and evaluations.

Dr. Henderson has distinguished himself among his peers and enjoys the respect of his professional associates, as evidenced by his election to the position of Chairman of Psychiatry at three major District of Columbia hospitals. His pursuit toward these distinguished career achievements began at Magnolia High School in Vicksburg, MS, where he was valedictorian of the Class of 1941. He earned a scholarship to Morehouse College where he graduated with highest honors in 1944 with a then unparalleled "first." He completed his academic requirements in three years instead of the traditional four, held a dual major in physics and mathematics, and still earned a perfect 4.0 grade point average.

As a physician Dr. Henderson challenged the racial structure and institutions of the city of McKeesport, Pennsylvania, where he was the first black intern/resident. There he organized a chapter of the NAACP and served as its first president. Under his leadership, black citizens in that city were first hired at local department stores, hospitals, public schools, and police and fire departments.

Having been listed in Who's Who in America, Dr. Henderson is one of the earliest black physicians to enter the field of psychiatry, and is one of the first psychiatrists to analyze the psychodynamics of racism. Dr. Henderson is one of six children of the late Rev. James H. and Charlotte Henderson. His wife of thirty-five years is the former Shirley S. Statom, the current and first African American president of the Women's National Democratic Club. They have four children and two grandchildren.

Marvin A. Jackson, M.D.
PROFESSOR OF PATHOLOGY
College of Medicine
Howard University
Washington, D.C.

Dr. Jackson finished Morehouse in 1947 and received his M.D. from Meharry in 1951. He went on to get an M.A. from the University of Michigan in 1956. He did a residency in Pathology at University Hospital, University of Michigan, Ann Arbor, and another one in Orthopedic Pathology at the Hospital for Joint Disease, New York. He has written thirty-three articles and supplied chapters for popular medical books. Dr. Jackson is certified to practice in Michigan and the District of Columbia. Currently, he is Professor of Pathology in the Howard University College of Medicine. He has held teaching positions at the University of Michigan; University of Glasgow, Scotland; and a visiting professorship at the College of Medicine, University of Maiduguri, Nigeria.

From Dr. Jackson's thirty-three publications, we list a sampling of the more recent titles of research projects in which he has been a contributor with others:

Jackson, M.A. "Factors Involved in the High Incidence of Prostatic Cancer Among Blacks." Eds. C. Mettlin and G. P. Murphy. Cancer Among Black Populations. New York: Alan R. Liss, 1981. 111-132.

—. Characterization of Prostatic Carcinoma Among Blacks: A Comparison Between a Low-incidence Area, Ibadan, Nigeria, and a high-incidence area, Washington, D.C., U.S.A. Prostate 1 (1980):185-205.

—. Blood Hormonc Profiles in Prostate Cancer Patients in High-risk and Low-risk Populations. Cancer 48 (1981): 2267- 2273.

—. Cancer of the Prostate and Aging: An Autopsy Study in Black Men From Washington, D.C. and Selected African Cities. Prostate 3 (1982): 73-80.

—. Ductal spread in prostatic carcinoma. Cancer 56(8) (1985): 1566-1573.

—. The role of diet in prostate cancer. Nutr. Cancer 9 (1087): 123-128.

Rudolph E. Jackson, M.D.
PROFESSOR OF PEDIATRICS
Morehouse School of Medicine
Atlanta, Georgia

No Photo Available

Dr. Jackson finished Morehouse in 1957 and Meharry in 1961. He interned at Homer G. Phillips Hospital, St. Louis, Missouri, and spent two years as a medical officer in the U.S. Navy. He did his residency at the U. S. Navy and Children's Hospital in Philadelphia, PA. He was Assistant Member in Hematology, St. Jude's Children's Research Hospital. He served as Assistant Professor of Pediatrics, University of Tennessee, Memphis, TN and later Program Coordinator, National Sickle Cell Disease Program and Chief, Sickle Cell Disease Branch, National Institutes of Health,Washington, D.C. He was Professor and Chairman, Department of Pediatrics, Meharry Medical College, Nashville, TN and Clinical Professor, Department of Allied Health, Trevecca Nazarene College in Nashville.

Between 1984 and 1990, Dr. Jackson was Professor and Acting Chairman, Department of Pediatrics, Morehouse School of Medicine, Atlanta. Since 1990 he has served there as Principal Investigator,Association of Minority Health Professions Schools AIDS Prevention Program. He also directs the USAID/Zambia HIV/AIDS Prevention Program there.

Dr. Jackson has published twenty-four abstracts,twenty-three articles, and has made over 200 scientific presentations.

Edward A. Jones, Jr., M.D.
PULMONARY SPECIALIST
Grand Rapids, Michigan

No Photo Available

Dr. Jones, a second generation Morehouse man, finished Morehouse in 1949 and received the M.D. at Meharry in 1955. He did an internship at Cincinnati General Hospital in Cincinnati, Ohio, and a residency in internal medicine at the same institution. Since 1975 he has been in private practice with Pulmonary Associates of Western Michigan, in Grand Rapids, Michigan. He has served as Associate Director of the Cardiopulmonary Department at St. Mary's Hospital in Grand Rapids, as Medical Coordinator there, and on the staff of the Free Bed Hospital and Rehabilitation Center in Grand Rapids.

Dr. Jones indicates on his returned questionnaire that he knew that several Morehouse students received assistance from Dr. Mays but did not know their names. Nor was he certain at first that he was among them. Of one thing he is certain, though; he was not told at the time. And he is sure of another thing: "Dr. Mays inspired all of us to be concerned about mankind."

Dr. E.A. Jones, Jr. has had medical appointments other than those mentioned above, all of them too in Grand Rapids. Among them are the following: Acting Consulting Staff Member, Department of Pulmonary Medicine with major privileges, St. Mary's Hospital;

Courtesy Staff Attending Physician, Ferguson Hospital; Courtesy Staff, Butterworth Hospital. Having had eighteen post-graduate medical experiences in thirteen different cities, he is a member of the Grand Rapids NAACP., a past board member of the Grand Rapids Urban League; a current board member of the Southeast Y.M.C.A., Opera Grand Rapids, and Grand Rapids Art Museum. He was president of Freedom Homes, Inc., which built twelve new homes in inner city Grand Rapids. He was a recipient of the Grand Rapids Bar Association Liberty Bell Award; the NAACP. Floyd Skinner Award; the Eugene Browning Medical Service Award Giant's Banquet; and an Outstanding Community Leadership and Service Award.

Dr. Jones belongs to six medical societies. He is married to Mrs. Harriet Sims Jones. They have three children.

Perry P. Little, D.D.
DENTIST
High Point, N.C.

No Photo Available

According to the Morehouse College Alumni Directory, Dr. Little finished Morehouse in 1948 and Meharry in 1952. He practices dentistry in High Point, North Carolina. Dr. Little's returned questionnaire indicates that he completed Meharry in 1952, gaining Mays-Mitchell help over the four year period. About that financial assistance he makes he commented: "In later years I knew of Dr. Mays's help."

He also knew, apparently, of help given to Drs. Clarence Littlejohn and the man he calls 'Will Shoot' Smith. He adds, "I was surprised and gratified that the race problem did not prevent Dr. Mays and Ms. Mitchell from working together for Morehouse men who needed help." He concludes with the lesson he learned, "One should always give back more than he receives."

Dr. Little has been an active participant in the Civil Rights Movement in North Carolina, serving as president of the local NAACP chapter in his city of residence. He is married and the father of three children.

Clarence G. Littlejohn, M.D.
Pediatric Cardiologist
Los Angeles, CA

Dr. Littlejohn finished Morehouse in 1949 and Meharry in 1953. His internship was done at the Hospital of San Raphael, New Haven, Connecticut, and his residency at Children's Hospital, Philadelphia, PA. He has served as Acting Head and Assistant Head of Pediatrics, Cardiology Lab, Children's Hospital, Los Angeles, California. Since 1958 he has been Clinical Assistant Professor of Pediatric Cardiology at the University of Southern California School of Medicine, Los Angeles. Since 1961 he has been Pediatric Cardiologist at the Watts Health Foundation and in private practice in Los Angeles.

In his returned questionnaire, Dr. Littlejohn indicates that he did know that he and Dr. Otis Smith were recipients of financial aid from Dr. Mays and Margaret Mitchell. In fact he tells us that Dr. Mays requested that he write a letter of thanks to Ms. Mitchell's husband. A copy of Dr. Littlejohn's letter to Mr. Marsh, dated October 14, 1951, follows:

Dear Mr. Marsh:

Introducing myself, I am Clarence Littlejohn, junior medical student of Meharry Medical College and 1949 graduate of Morehouse

College in Atlanta. I was one of the recipients of the scholarship aid made possible thru Morehouse College by the generosity and understanding of your wife, Mrs. Margaret Mitchell Marsh. Dr. Mays has acquainted me with the exemplary spirit she displayed by establishing such a fund to be used to aid young students of medicine who plan to practice in the South.

I am indeed grateful for the admirable deed your wife did and wish to show my appreciation — for such aid came to me when a financial crisis threatened the financial structure of my medical education. My anemic resources had begun sagging, and I was spending much of my time (which should have been allotted to studies) racking my brain trying to think of ways and means to pull myself out of my financial rut. Strangely enough, there are few scholarships offered to medical students, I found out upon applying to many. And working after school (like I did at Morehouse) is out of the question if you want to learn at least 3/4 of the material tossed at you in texts and classrooms. So you see, the scholarship aid was a life saver. I shall do my utmost to prove myself worthy of having received it.

Thanks. With kindest regards, I am

Very truly yours,

Clarence G. Littlejohn

Sere MYERS, Sr.
ORAL SURGEON
Kansas City, Missouri

Dr. Sere S. Myers, Sr. entered Morehouse College as a fifteen (15) year old early admission student in the Fall of 1946. He graduated after earning the B.S. degree in 1950. He served in the U. S. Army during the Korean War, 1951-1953, and after his internship, enlisted in the U.S. Air Force, where he served from 1959-1961 as Chief of Dental Surgery at Forbes Air Force Base, Topeka, Kansas.

After graduating from Morehouse, and prior to his first enlistment, Myers enrolled in the Howard University School of Dentistry, where he earned the D.D. degree in 1958.

Dr. Myers is a mentor, community and professional activist and a positive force in Kansas City and the medical profession because of his commitment to providing quality dental services to the inner city and impoverished communities in Kansas City. He is also active in numerous organizations, including: the Howard University Alumni Association, the Morehouse College Alumni Association, the Urban League, the NAACP, the National Dental Association, the American Dental Association, the Kansas City and Missouri Dental Associations, Kappa Alpha Psi Fraternity, Sigma Pi Phi Fraternity, and is a member of the Board of Directors of the Douglass State Bank.

In his response to our inquiry, he said of Dr. Mays: "At the age of fifteen, my first year at Morehouse, Dr. Mays' speeches sent chills down my spine. He made us feel that if we could succeed at Morehouse, we could conquer the outside world. When he walked among us, it was like a Messiah had entered the room."

Dr. Myers concluded that Dr. Mays helped him both financially and with his words of encouragement and wisdom during his years at Morehouse and Howard. He remembers most some of the wisdom of Dr. Mays, such as:

> *Morehouse can prepare you. If you make an "A" at Morehouse, you can make an "A" at Harvard. If you make a "B" at Morehouse, you can make a "B" at Oxford.*
>
> *I do not dislike Notre Dame -- but I love Morehouse because it is mine.*

Dr. Myers is married to the former Mary Jane Stewart. They have five children.

Otis W. Smith, M.D.
Pediatrician
College Park, Georgia

Otis Wesley Smith was born on May 12, 1925 in Atlanta, Georgia. Growing up in the Vine City Community in Atlanta, young Otis' home was situated adjacent to the Morris Brown College campus. He attended the Ashby Street Elementary School and Booker T. Washington High School.

After enrolling in Morehouse College, Smith lettered in four sports and earned the nickname "Will Shoot" because of his feats in basketball. He later played on a YMCA team, the City Slickers, with Martin Luther King, Jr. as a teammate. Following his 1947 graduation from Morehouse, Smith earned a masters degree at Atlanta University and entered medical school at Meharry School of Medicine in 1950. He was awarded the M.D. in 1954.

Dr. Smith interned at the Homer G. Phillips Hospital in St. Louis, Missouri from 1954-1955, completed his residency there from 1958 to 1961 and served as Chief of Pediatric from 1961-1964. He practiced medicine as a Pediatrician in Atlanta from 1964 until his retirement in 1987.

In medicine, Dr. Smith became the first Black physician certified by the American Academy of Pediatrics to practice in

Georgia, where he practiced for more than forty years. A leader in the field of medical advancements for children, Smith served as doctor, friend, mentor and father-figure for at least two generations of Atlanta families who came to depend on "Dr. O. S." for sound medical assistance and advice.

A community activist, Dr. Smith was a leader in the desegregation of Atlanta hospitals. Along with a group of national leaders, he was instrumental in the desegration of hospitals throughout the country. This involvement was highlighted in an invitation from the Department of Health, Education and Welfare to attend a White House announcement of the integration of all of the nation's hospitals.

In addition to his outstanding career in medicine, Dr. Smith has been a leader in the area of civil and human rights and the struggles for justice and equality in the city of Atlanta and the state of Georgia. He was elected president of the Atlanta Chapter of the National Association for the Advancement of Colored People.

Smith is a lifetime member of the NAACP, the Alpha Phi Alpha Fraternity, the Butler Street YMCA, the Atlanta Medical Association, the National Medical Association and the West Fulton Rotary. Continuing a pattern of service to humanity, his appointments during the past half centry have included: Vice Chair, Board of Directors, West End Medical Center; Member, Board of Trustee, St. Mark AME Church, a church founded by his grandfather; Member, Board of Trustees, Turner Theological Seminary, Interdenominational Theological Center; Member, Advisory Board, Morehouse College; Treasurer, local chapter, Southern Christian Leadership Conference; Chairman, Implementation Committee of the Atlanta Medical Association; Chair/Co-chair, Atlanta Health Care Task Force; Chairman, Atlanta Summit Leadership Conference; Alumni Member, Board of Management, Meharry Medical College; Member, Board of Directors, Sickle Cell Foundation; Member, Board of Directors, Southside Comprehensive Health Center; Member, Fulton-Dekalb Hospital Authority and Member, Board of Directors and Vice-chairman, Margaret Mitchell House, Inc.

As a result of his humanitarian and philanthropic contributions, Smith has emulated his mentor, Dr. Benjamin E. Mays, for more than fifty years and has received countless recognitions for his service to his communities. Among them are: the first recipient of the Benjamin E. Mays Service Award at Morehouse College (1989); the Turner Broadcasting "Trumpet Award" for outstanding community service (1985); the Atlanta Medical Association's "Physician of the Year Award" (1969 and 1983); the NAACP Freedom Hall of Fame and the Nash-Carter Award (1989).

Organizations that have cited him include: Ebony Magazine, Fortune Magazine, Jet Magazine, the Southwest Community Hospital, the Georgia State Medical Association, the 100% Wrong Club; the Georgia House of Representatives and the Georgia State Medical Association.

Dr. Smith and his wife Gwen have one son and one grandson.

Artis A. White, D.D.
DENTIST
Inglewood, California

No Photo Available

Dr. White finished Morehouse in 1951 and Meharry in 1955. He speaks of knowing that he received a total of about $2000 in aid to help him during his first and second years of medical school. His first reaction when he learned of the aid was "Buck Bennie Rides Again!! He has given, as he modestly states in his questionnaire, many charitable contributions. He reported, for example, that he has arranged for Morehouse to benefit from a bequest of $1,000,000.

The Mitchell Scholars as Students

by Dr. Calvin L. Calhoun, Sr
Retired Professor of Anatomy
Meharry College of Medicine

Dr. Calvin L. Calhoun, Sr., a Morehouse alumnus (1948) and retired professor of Meharry, taught several of those who were recipients and attended Meharry. He identifies the ones he taught as being Drs. Delmar Edwards, Clarence Littlejohn, Marvin Jackson, Rudolph Jackson, and E.A. Jones, Jr. He had no knowledge of the Mitchell funds until learning of the program from Johnson within the last two years.

Because of Dr. Calhoun's lengthy career at Meharry, he is able to write, "I had a first hand relationship with the Morehouse alumni in medical and dental studies. Most of them became health care deliverers...in inner city areas. Dr. Calhoun continues:

> *I saw them as highly motivated and energetic young men who studied with diligence. The fact that they could not get public accommodations, had to drink from "colored" water fountains, ride in the front car of trains, among the cinders and smoke, or the back of street cars and busses behind white passengers did not deter them or make them lose their self esteem nourished at Morehouse College under Dr. Mays.*

> *Besides the sorts of barriers listed above, they found at Meharry a constantly rigorous academic regimen, with no campus dormitories, but with financial requirements for each year to be paid before the next one began. They*

mostly came from non-affluent families, and there was little time available for employment. Tuition for the 1948-49 class was $475.00 plus $60.00 in various fees.

Tuition 'in full' was required at the beginning of each quarter before the student could attend classes. In 1951-52 tuition was $575.00. For comparative purposes, tuition in 1975 was $2500 per year when my son, Calvin Jr., a Morehouse graduate, finished Meharry and was $16,500 in 1995 with up to $2000 in various fees.

Hence, the incalculable value of the motivation and financial assistance from Dr. Mays and Mrs. Mitchell becomes apparent.

Dr. Calhoun, who taught at Morehouse a while, tells us that Dr. Mays was his "ideal thinker" and adds,

His encouragement to be all you can regardless of circumstances, his teaching us of the equality of men, and the need to protest against segregation (even if silently) motivated me throughout my life and career. Mrs. Mays, Mrs. Thelma Archer, Mrs. Lamar, and other wives at Morehouse took in the wives of young staff members and taught them the social graces.

The Calhouns' affinity to the Mays spirit led them to establish an Emergency Student Loan Fund at Morehouse College in 1993 and at Meharry in 1995.

IV
THE AFTERWORD

The search for meaning in Margaret Mitchell's philanthropic largess to Mays's Morehouse men leads to a search in the annals of American history and the depths of man's humanity. Why would the daughter of the Confederate South aid descendants of slaves? The question is really grounded in Biblical wisdom, "Can anything good come out of Nazareth"? This question, ringing in minds of the Philistines, the Canaanites, and even some Nazarenes, challenged the deity, sanctity, and holy supremacy of the man who hailed from the little fishing village of Nazareth. Some in Mays's day might too have questioned the veracity and depth of any possible commitment of a daughter of the Confederate South to a man who hailed from an unknown town named Ninety Six, South Carolina. Would Morehouse College, still a bastion of black intellect, however needy, be required to sacrifice its principles for monetary gain? After all, Gone With The Wind had never rated high on black people's lists of favorite books to read or movies to watch from the small number of hot, dirty balconies in southern movie houses that admitted Blacks. Mays had the idea that Mitchell might help, and so she did. The Mitchell-Mays connection bore plentiful fruit.

In his autobiography, Mays wrote about Mitchell's help to Morehouse College: "There are, of course, good and happy memories that should be told. One such concerns Margaret Mitchell. Countless thousands associate her name with Gone With The Wind; But Morehouse men have a very special association with her. Not infrequently have Negro servants willed what little they have to white people for whom they worked. When Margaret Mitchell's devoted servant willed several thousands of dollars to her, Miss Mitchell gave it to Morehouse to be used for needy, worthy black students. The money was used to aid Morehouse graduates in their struggle through medical school. Since Margaret Mitchell was not inclined to proclaim her acts of generosity, I am glad to record this one here" (212). The servant was Carrie Mitchell Holbrook.

Can any good come out of Nazareth? The resounding answer, now, as in Biblical times, is YES. Whether Nazareth is a two mule shack in racially segregated South Carolina or a comfortable bungalow in racially segregated Georgia, Nazareth is still the workplace of a God who sees all and heals all. We have seen here the workings of God and man and woman in uplifting the downtrodden, in bringing hope to the weary, in bringing unity to the divided.

Atlanta is the beneficiary. At every major juncture in Atlanta's modern history, Blacks and Whites, women and men, have made a collective effort to co-exist as neighbors and cooperate as partners on matters considered to be of mutual interest to the city. Since World War II, this southern metropolis has avoided the racial divisiveness that scarred Birmingham, Selma, Montgomery, many parts of Mississippi, and other places. Let there be no mistake. The imposition of white primaries and Jim Crow laws in Atlanta and the state of Georgia were just as painful, cruel, degrading and dehumanizing as Sheriff Bill Clark's firehoses in Mississippi and Bull Connor's dogs in Birmingham.

Man's inhumanity to man always robs the weaker one of his human dignity and respect but robs the other of the basic moral decency required to be truly human. White Atlantans may have been <u>just</u> as fervent in their personal dislike for Blacks and the racial progress made by Blacks as were their Confederate cousins in the mountains of Tennessee. However, the decision by the leadership in this city to find ways to comply with federal mandates ensuring equal rights to Blacks and not exploit racial bigotry was not only humane but made good economic sense. Atlanta had finally realized that to hold the black man down in the ditch the white man had to be down there too.

It is not by accident that the Atlanta Braves are not the Birmingham Barons; the Falcons are not in Nashville; the Hawks are not wearing the jerseys of Jackson, Mississippi; and the nation's busiest airport is not contributing to the tax base of either North or South Carolina. Fifty years before Antonio Samaranch, head of the international Olympic organization, could proclaim to the world "It's Atlanta!!!" the seeds of racial harmony had already been sown by people like Margaret Mitchell and Benjamin Mays. Before Billy Payne and Andrew Young could bring the world to Atlanta's door as athletes from 109 nations competing for Olympic gold; before William Hartsfield, Ivan Allen, Maynard Jackson, Andrew Young, and Bill Campbell could present to the world "A city too busy to hate;" before Mills B. Lane set his considerable C&S wealth in motion for the development of downtown Atlanta, including the Fulton County Stadium as a prerequisite for luring the Milwaukee Braves; before Ralph McGill penned his first column of brilliant prose trumpeting racial justice from the front page of the Atlanta Constitution; before Robert Woodruff as "Mr. Anonymous" and his Coca-Cola millions became synonymous with building a better Atlanta; before John Portman could raise his atriums and revolving lounges; before Sweet Auburn could meet Smooth Peachtree, Benjamin Mays and Margaret Mitchell were already there. They showed Atlanta, and indeed the South, the road map to the black and white racial harmony that exists today.

Mays and Mitchell did not join forces to help some deserving students realize their dreams to become doctors merely to enhance the wealth of selected individuals; nor were their collaborative efforts the result of subliminal ambition merely to see Morehouse College become great, prestitious, or popular. The Mays-Mitchell connection had its very root in a genuine commitment to uplift a people who suffered a serious shortage of doctors needed to heal their sick and a hospital where a black minority could have a chance to recuperate from their illnesses or at least "to die in dignity." Indeed, by their example, which was little known, and that of many others who are well known, Mays and Mitchell showed Atlanta the way.

WORKS CITED

Alexander, T.M. Beyond The Timberline: The Trials and Triumph of A Black Entrepreneur. Edgewater,MD: Duncker & Company, 1942.

Bennett, Lerone, Jr. "The Last of the Great Schoolmasters." Ebony 32. Dec. 1977: 74-79.

Burton, Orville Vernon. Quoted in Foreword to Born to Rebel. New York: Charles Scribner's Sons, 1971.

Carter, Lawrence E., ed. Walking Integrity: Benjamin E. Mays, Mentor to Generations. Atlanta: Scholars Press, 1996.

Cook, Samuel Dubois. "A Memorial Tribute to Dr. Benjamin E. Mays." The Atlanta Inquirer. 28 April,1984.

Edwards, Anne. Road to Tara: The Life of Margaret Mitchell, Author of Gone With The Wind. New Haven: Ticknor & Fields, 1983.

Farr, Finis. Margaret Mitchell of Atlanta, the Author of Gone With The Wind: Her Story. New York: William Morrow, 1965.

Franklin, John Hope and Alfred A. Moss, Jr. From Slavery to Freedom. 7th ed. New York: McGraw-Hill, 1994.

Garrett, Franklin. Atlanta and Environs: A Chronicle of Its People and Events. New York: Lewis Historical Publishing, 1954.

Harwell, Richard. ed. Margaret Mitchell's "Gone With The Wind" Letters: 1936-1939. New York: Macmillan, 1976.

Hornsby, Alton, Jr. Chronology of African American History: Significant Events and People from 1619 to the Present. Detroit: Gale Research, 1991.

Jones, E.A. A Candle in the Dark: A History of Morehouse College. Valley Forge: Judson, 1967.

Mays, Benjamin E. Born to Rebel. New York: Charles Scribner's Sons, 1971.

----. Quotable Quotes of Benjamin E. Mays. New York: Vantage Press, 1983.

Mitchell, Margaret. Gone With The Wind. New York: Macmillan, 1936.

Pyron, Darden Asbury. Southern Daughter: The Life of Margaret Mitchell. New York: Oxford University Press, 1991.

Roddenbery, S. A. I Swear By Apollo: A Black Surgeon in the Deep South. Hamilton, GA: Grandy Press, 1994.

Rovaris, Dereck J. Mays and Morehouse: How Benjamin E. Mays Developed Morehouse College, 1940-1967. Silver Spring: Becham House, 1990.

Walker, Marianne. Margaret Mitchell and John Marsh: The Love Story Behind Gone With The Wind. Atlanta: Peachtree, 1993.

ABOUT THE AUTHORS

IRA JOE JOHNSON

Ira Joe Johnson is a graduate of Morehouse College, where he served as a student member of the College's Board of Trustees and a writer for the student newspaper. He attended Columbia Southern College of Law.

A longtime government official, civil rights activist and political adviser, he has served on the staffs of Atlanta mayors Maynard Jackson and Andrew Young and in the administrations of former presidents Jimmy Carter and Bill Clinton. Johnson was appointed to the Georgia Youth Council under former Georgia governor, Jimmy Carter. He has also served as Senior Political Campaign Advisor for Senator Ted Kennedy and as Director of Public Affairs for the Mayflower Group, the telecommunications company owned by Attorney Johnny Cochran.

Johnson is the author of the 1980 series, Blacks and the Carter Presidency. His writings have appeared in several newspapers and magazines and he is in-demand as a public speaker and lecturer. He was a reporter for the Atlanta Voice newspaper while attending Morehouse College.

As a close associate of Dr. Mays from 1972 to 1984, Johnson was active in his campaign and election to the Atlanta Board of Education and travelled with him as his assistant and protege throughout those years. Dr. Mays was the Godfather of his son, Ira Joe, Jr.

Johnson is married to the former Ruby Wright and is the father of three children.

ABOUT THE AUTHORS

WILLIAM G. PICKENS

William G. Pickens, Ph.D., a native Atlantan, graduated magna cum laude and Phi Beta Kappa from Morehouse College in 1948. He later earned the doctorate at the University of Connecticut.

A professor of literature and linguistics at Morehouse College and former visiting professor at Emory University, Dr. Pickens was named a "Distinguished Faculty Scholar" by the United Negro College Fund.

DUE DATE